14

W9-AXC-150

ONE REHEARSAL PAGEANTS

PAGEANTS

for the

CHURCH

By

HARRY W. GITHENS

THE STANDARD PUBLISHING COMPANY
CINCINNATI, O.

Contents

Introduction

In these days of so many activities which take the time of nearly every one connected with the church, it usually is difficult to assemble even a small group for a few rehearsals of a play, pageant or other entertainment. Many splendid educational programs have been published, but the average church feels they are too difficult, and people will not give time for rehearsals. Furthermore, in pageants where there are many speakers, their voices do not always carry, and the effect of the message is lost. It is to meet these conditions that this volume has been prepared.

In most of these pageants the story is given by one or more readers, while the scenes are presented in tableau or pantomime. In every case there must be careful preparation of costumes and scenery. Some of these pageants may be rehearsed in the afternoon and presented the same evening; but for the heavier pageants it is recommended that the rehearsal be held at least twenty-four hours before the presentation, to allow time for altering costumes and making minor changes.

America's Hour*

A PAGEANT OF CHRISTIAN LIBERTY AND BROTHERHOOD

CHARACTERS

SPIRIT OF BROTHERHOOD.

LIBERTY.

JUSTICE.

FOUR TRUMPETERS.

EGYPT.

BABYLONIA.

GREECE.

ROME.

AMERICA.

INDIAN.

NEGRO.

PIONEER.

IMMIGRANTS.

ORIENTALS.

CHOIR.

HERALD.

COSTUMES

SPIRIT OF BROTHERHOOD.

Soft white gown, reaching to ankles and girded at waist. Wreath of leaves around head and also over left shoulder. Carries a scroll made from brown wrapping-paper, on which her lines are pasted or written. The scroll should unroll from left to right.

LIBERTY.

White gown similar to BROTHERHOOD's, with bandings of old gold and cape of old-gold-colored sateen hung from left shoulder. Spiked crown of gold. Carries a torch (flashlight with red paper flame) in right hand, and an eighteen-inch gilded cardboard cross in left hand, concealed under cape until time to display.

---

* Adapted from "The Striking of America's Hour," published by the Woman's Missionary Society of the United Lutheran Church in America, 1228 Spruce St., Philadelphia, and used by permission.

JUSTICE.

White robe similar to BROTHERHOOD's, with cape of purple sateen. Carries scales made by gilding two paper plates which are fastened to a gilded rod by gilt cords.

TRUMPETERS.

Knee-length dresses of yellow cheesecloth, with full sleeves. Black girdle and black bands around arms. Yellow band around head. Carry trumpets of gilded cardboard.

EGYPT.

Long gown of nile-green cheesecloth, with Egyptian headdress, jeweled stomacher, bracelets and beads.

BABYLONIA.

Loose costume of brown, red and green stripes. Lace veil fastened with jeweled bands or beads. Beads and buckles for ornaments.

GREECE.

Conventional Grecian costume of soft material, girded at waist, and hair arranged in psyche style, with filet about head.

ROME.

Yellow or orange robe, with girdle and sash of purple. Crown with eagle ornament, gilded.

AMERICA.

White dress with drapery of bunting and cap also of the bunting material.

PIONEER OR PILGRIM.

Brown smock and knee breeches, black stockings, bedroom slippers; large, soft, white collar with bow tie; soft felt hat.

INDIAN.

Characteristic Indian dress.

NEGRO.

Plain suit or dress.

IMMIGRANTS.

Representing several European nations. Women wear bright shawls over heads and carry packs; some are leading small children. Men in overalls, carrying picks and shovels.

ORIENTALS.

> Representatives from China, India, Japan, Africa and Moslem lands. See costumes described in "The Torch Bearers."

CHOIR.

> May wear surplices or white robes and carry palms or ferns.

HERALD.

> Plain white dress, with headband of white ribbon.

ARRANGEMENT

The platform should have a throne arranged at rear center for SPIRIT OF BROTHERHOOD, LIBERTY and JUSTICE. Greenery may be banked around the base of the platform.

PAGEANT

TRUMPET [*in distance*]—"God of Our Fathers, Whose Almighty Hand."

HERALD [*enters and raises right hand to secure attention*]—Hark, O ye people, we come to spread before you a pageant of today. In music and color and motion, we shall paint you a canvas which shall tell a story of this world.

Heed well the words of the central figure—the Spirit of Brotherhood—who, since time began, has dwelt upon this earth, supported by Liberty and Justice. Before these three, see the nations of the past summoned for judgment. Last of all, behold America appear before the judgment seat. Hear the pleas of foreign lands, for life and light. Let imagination paint for you the moving drama of world history and let conscience repeat in your ears the great chords intoned by the multitude of voices which, in every language spoken on the earth today, are sounding forth the striking of America's hour.

CHOIR PROCESSIONAL—"God of Our Fathers, Whose Almighty Hand," or "Lead On, O King Eternal."

FOUR TRUMPETERS—[*two enter right and two left, blow summons at center front, then step back, two on each side, while* SPIRIT OF BROTHERHOOD *enters, right front. (Cornetist behind scenes may give bugle call when trumpeters raise their trumpets to lips.) The* SPIRIT OF BROTHERHOOD *ascends to central throne while pianist plays a few strains from "Pilgrims Chorus," or appropriate march*].

SPIRIT OF BROTHERHOOD [*raising right hand*]—Summon Liberty and Justice, so that I, the Spirit of Brotherhood, may have their counsel.

TRUMPETERS—[*face front and sound call, then step back as before, forming aisle, as* LIBERTY *and* JUSTICE *enter, one from right and one from left front, and take their places on either side of* BROTHERHOOD, *accompanied by piano strains as before*].

SPIRIT OF BROTHERHOOD—Upon this planet, Earth, man has dwelt for many thousand years. He has made fire and stone, ivory and iron, to do his will. Upon the walls of caves, which were his earliest home, he has carved the record of his conquests. World kingdoms have risen and world kingdoms have perished. From each of them an account shall be required. First of the mighty world powers, Egypt, answer the summons. Trumpeters, call Egypt.

TRUMPETERS—[*face front and sound call, then step back as before*].

EGYPT—[*enters from right, bows before* SPIRIT OF BROTHERHOOD, *and stands, waiting. Choir sings for entrance of Egypt the first verse of "Before Jehovah's Awful Throne"*].

SPIRIT OF BROTHERHOOD—Egypt, first of mighty nations, in the name of Liberty, Justice and Brotherhood, thou art summoned to judgment.

EGYPT—Five thousand years ago my ships left the shelter of the Nile and crossed the Mediterranean and Ægean Seas, bearing foreign captives and foreign gold for my great Pharaohs. With copper mines in Sinai and caravans in Sudan bringing ivory, ebony and incense; with my looms weaving linen finer than silk; my slaves building mighty pyramids and giant columns; my artists making wondrous portraits and statues; my lapidaries cutting magnificent jewels; my priests skilled in science and in arts, great was my power.

SPIRIT OF BROTHERHOOD—Great *was* thy power, O Egypt, but, as a voice from a glory departed, speak thy pyramids on the Nile. They are monuments not only of thy Pharaohs' power, but of their reckless contempt for human life. To build these tombs of greatness, thousand of slaves toiled, fainting and dying under the taskmaster's scourge. Thy obelisks have fallen or been carried to the museums of other lands. Thy portraits and statues have crumbled to dust.

JUSTICE [*raising scales*]—Egypt, thou art weighed in the balances and found wanting.

LIBERTY [*raising torch*]—Thou didst not set thy people free.

SPIRIT OF BROTHERHOOD—The one true God thou didst reject. Thou didst not send out the true light to lighten the world. Pass on!

[EGYPT *exits with bowed head, or takes her place at rear of stage while choir sings first verse of, "O Where Are Kings and Empires Now?"*]

SPIRIT OF BROTHERHOOD—The unresting ages pass on. Another world empire rules the earth. From the Nile to the Tigris-Euphrates goes the scepter of empire. Babylonia, answer the summons.

TRUMPETERS—[*face front and sound call, then step back as before*].

BABYLONIA—[*enters from left, bows before* SPIRIT OF BROTHERHOOD, *and stands waiting, while choir sings first verse of,* "*Before Jehovah's Awful Throne*"].

SPIRIT OF BROTHERHOOD—Babylonia, in the name of Liberty, Justice and Brotherhood, thou art summoned to judgment.

BABYLONIA—Upon the Plain of Shinar in ancient Nippur rose the Temple Mount of the Sumerian god of the air. With wealth brought from many lands were built my lofty towers of tessellated brick. At the whim of a woman, thousands of lash-driven slaves made my hanging gardens. To the greatest of my kings was given power and strength and glory. He had his den of lions and his fiery furnace. All nations trembled before him. Whom he would, he slew, and whom he would, he kept alive.

SPIRIT OF BROTHERHOOD—Great *was* thy power, O Babylonia, and thy heart was lifted up and thy mind hardened with pride. So it was that all thy magicians and astrologers and soothsayers were not able to save thee from thy doom. Thou didst praise the gods of silver, of gold and of brass, but the God in whose hand thy breath is, and whose are all thy ways, thou didst not glorify. Thy day of opportunity is past.

JUSTICE [*raising scales*]—Thou art weighed in the balances and found wanting.

LIBERTY—Thou didst not set thy people free.

[BABYLONIA *takes her place beside* EGYPT, *while choir sings first verse of,* "*O Where Are Kings and Empires Now?*"]

SPIRIT OF BROTHERHOOD—For many generations the mountains were clothed in green and bared again. Another world kingdom rises upon the earth. Greece, mightiest of all world empires, answer the summons.

TRUMPETERS—[*face front and sound call, then step back as before*].

GREECE—[*enters from right, bows before* SPIRIT OF BROTHERHOOD, *and stands waiting, while choir sings first verse of, "Before Jehovah's Awful Throne"*].

SPIRIT OF BROTHERHOOD—Greece, in the name of Liberty, Justice and Brotherhood, thou art summoned to judgment.

GREECE—The mighty monuments which tell of my glory are the wonder of the world. In imperishable marble my great artists have fixed the dreams of beauty for which men have died. My poets and philosophers gave the world a new idea of freedom which shall live forever in the hearts of men. Why is my dominion gone? Why has my glory departed?

SPIRIT OF BROTHERHOOD—O Greece, never was nation greater than thou in thy love of beauty and of freedom. But thy markets were filled with slaves. Thy women were untaught. In the multitude of thy gods and in the splendor of thy temples, thou didst not see the Lord of heaven and earth who dwelleth not in temples made with hands.

JUSTICE [*raising scales*]—Thou art weighed in the balances and found wanting.

LIBERTY—Thou didst not set thy people free.

SPIRIT OF BROTHERHOOD—Thou didst not send out the true light to lighten the world.

[GREECE *departs with bowed head and takes her place beside* BABYLONIA *and* EGYPT, *while choir sings first verse of, "O Where Are Kings and Empires Now?"*]

SPIRIT OF BROTHERHOOD—In unending flight the earth circles around its sun. A new empire rises. Rome, mistress of the world, answer the summons.

TRUMPETERS—[*face front and sound call, then step back as before*].

ROME—[*enters from left, bows before* SPIRIT OF BROTHERHOOD, *and stands waiting, while choir sings first verse of,* "*Before Jehovah's Awful Throne*"].

SPIRIT OF BROTHERHOOD—Rome, in the name of Liberty, Justice and Brotherhood, thou art summoned to judgment.

ROME—From the Atlantic to the Euphrates, from England to Egypt, my emperors were worshiped as gods. I gave the world noble buildings, great industries and a golden age of law and order. The eagles which glittered in front of my unconquered legions were revered in the remotest corner of the earth.

SPIRIT OF BROTHERHOOD—Thou didst conquer the world, mighty Rome, but thou didst not conquer thyself. Thou didst despise thine own gods. Thou didst torture and crucify the teachers who would have saved thee. Thou wast corrupted by thine own wealth, drunk with the love of power and given over to pleasure.

JUSTICE [*raising scales*]—Thou art weighed in the balances and found wanting.

LIBERTY—Thou didst not set thy people free.

SPIRIT OF BROTHERHOOD—Thou didst not send out the true light to lighten the world.

[ROME *departs with bowed head and takes her place beside the other nations, while choir sings first verse of,* "*O Where Are Kings and Empires Now?*"]

SPIRIT OF BROTHERHOOD—Today, glorious among the nations, stands a land which is exalted until the eyes of all the earth are turned to her and the hearts of all peoples wait on her. Trumpeters, call America.

TRUMPETERS—[*face front and sound call, after which the choir sings,* "*The Battle Hymn of the Republic*"].

AMERICA—[*enters from right, bows before* SPIRIT OF BROTHERHOOD, *and stands waiting*].

SPIRIT OF BROTHERHOOD—America, in the name of Liberty, Justice and Brotherhood, thou art summoned to judgment.

AMERICA—

> I am America, speaking one tongue,
> Acting my epics before they are sung,
> Driving my rails from the palms to the snow,
> Through states that are greater than emperors know;
> Forty-eight states that are empires in might,
> But ruled by the will of one people tonight;
> Nerved as one body with network of steel,
> Merging their strength in one common weal.
> Brooking no poverty, mocking at Mars,
> Building my cities to talk with the stars.
> Thriving, increasing by myriads again
> 'Til even in numbers old Europe shall wane!
>
> —*From "The Avenue of Allies," by Alfred Noyes.*

SPIRIT OF BROTHERHOOD—America, thou art like a mighty tree, the height of which reacheth to the heavens and the sight thereof to the ends of the earth. Riches and honor are with thee. Thy sons and daughters bring thee honor. Thy garners are full and thy cattle bring forth thousands in the fields. Yet thou art not the first nation that has been lifted up and highly exalted. Upon the nations of the past sentence has been rendered, and thou, too, America, must be judged. Thou art greater than the empires of the past, for thy dominion is founded not upon conquest, but upon the dominance of great ideals. Throughout the earth thy name stands for justice and freedom. Thou art the hope of the world for the realization of the visions which are stirring the heart of humanity in every land. Dost thou not hear the voices that call thee? Are thine eyes holden that thou canst not see?

AMERICA [*sings, to the tune of "Der Tennebaum"*]—

> My own beloved, my native land,
> How fair, how strong your mountains stand!
> Fling high your banner of the free,
> The flag so dear to you, to me.
> It waves that war on earth may cease,
> It tells of liberty and peace.
> O banner dear, from out my heart
> My love for thee shall ne'er depart.
>
> Our nation's boast, "In God we trust,"
> Hath raised the bondman from the dust;
> In Him alone can men be free,
> In Him alone is liberty.
> For peace, good will, on land and sea,
> For world-wide love that makes men free,
> For brotherhood, from shore to shore
> Our flag shall wave for evermore.

> —*"The Flag of Good Will," by Mary Shafer Jones.*

INDIAN [*or group of Indians, entering while pianist plays "Red Wing"*]—Before thou wast called America, the red man dwelt in this great land. As thou hast advanced, we have been pressed back. The red man has ever given way to the white man. Liberty, Justice and Brotherhood, the Indians ask of thee the light of the white man's Book of heaven.

PIONEER [*or group of Pioneers, entering while pianist plays "America"*]—Not for us, America, was the soft couch of ease or the swift car of luxury. Through hard toil and ever-present danger we conquered thy soil, thy mountains, and thy rivers for the use of the generations that have come after us. Forget not the great hopes which brought us to thee. In the name of the resolute men who left their homes and kindred for the sake of political and religious freedom, I call upon thee to keep thine eyes unfalteringly fixed upon the ideals for which thy pioneers have fought and died.

NEGRO [*or group of Negroes, entering while pianist plays,* "*Way Down Upon the Suwanee River*"]—Not by our own choice are we here, America, the ten million Negroes in thy land. Yet we have builded our lives into the strength of America. We have marched forth to battle for the liberty of America and of the world. But think not that thou canst fulfill thy destiny by setting free the bodies of men so long as thou dost leave their minds enslaved by ignorance and superstition. We ask of thee the Justice of Christian Brotherhood, and the Liberty of mind and conscience set free.

IMMIGRANTS [*entering while pianist plays* "*Santa Lucia,*" *or other European folk song. One steps forward and speaks*] —O America, land of our dreams, from every land we come, seeking to find with thee freedom and light. Our hearts are beating in unison to a song of hope, a song of children playing in the light, a song of men going forth to battle against wrong, a song of mothers working in happy homes, a song of the "Stars and Stripes," waving over a land where no man is oppressed and where all eyes are upraised to God.

SPIRIT OF BROTHERHOOD—These are thine, America, who are building their lives into the greatness of thy land. Their picks dig the coal that runs the wheels of thy great industries. Their axes fell the trees that build thy homes and mighty ships. Yet many of them can not read the laws they are expected to obey, nor the orders issued for their protection. Unless thou dost give to them *thy* language, *thy* ideals, *thy* God, they will bring to thee *their* languages, *their* ideals, and *their* gods.

ORIENTALS—[*group representing China, India, Japan, Africa and Moslem lands, enters while choir sings one verse of,* "*From Greenland's Icy Mountains*"].

SPIRIT OF BROTHERHOOD—America, the hour of thine opportunity is striking, not only in thine own land, but in all the nations of the earth. From foreign lands in darkness, the call comes to thee for light.

CHINESE GIRL—America, China is breaking the shackles of superstition and custom. Our nation, long bound by the autocracy of the past, is stirring with hope for the future. Thy broad flag of liberty has once again spread its folds to protect us. Standing with unbound feet in the dawn of a new day, our women seek to be taught. Wilt thou not come to us with healing for bodies diseased and liberty for minds enslaved, and the light of the gospel for souls in darkness? The destiny of China waits upon thy answer.

INDIA—From India, caste-bound, priest-ridden, famine-swept India, I come. My people, millions of them, are doomed by caste to rise no higher than their fathers for many generations. If so much as the shadow of a man of low caste falls upon a man of higher birth, the latter must purge himself in the temple. India has millions of gods and yet we know not the true God. Wilt thou not send thy sons and daughters to tell us of the great Light?

JAPAN—America, thou hast opened thy ports to the world's commerce. Thou hast brought to us Western art and civilization. Our faith in our old gods is gone. Headless idols stand on our hillsides. Our universities are filled with teachers who scorn their old faith, but to them no new faith has been given. O America, speed thy messengers to Japan, the leader of the Orient, for the hour of thy opportunity is striking there as it has never struck before.

AFRICA—I bring from Africa a plea for Justice, Liberty and Light. Toiling in the white man's mines for the diamonds which sparkle in the banquet halls of lands our eyes shall never see, we have been degraded by the white man's rum and enslaved by his greed. Today Africa looks to America, pleading for the Light.

MOHAMMEDAN WOMAN—The hour strikes, America, when the cross meets the crescent. Which shall triumph? Shall we go back to the nameless horrors of Moslem harems? Hast thou no light which can pierce the veils of the women of Islam?

SPIRIT OF BROTHERHOOD [*designating all the Orientals*] —They wait before thee, America. In every land the hour of thy opportunity is striking.

JUSTICE—Thou shalt be weighed in the balances and found wanting, America,

LIBERTY—If thou dost not send out the true light to lighten the world.

HERALD—

Do you hear the people calling in the night?
In deep heathen darkness sighing for the light?
How their trembling hands uplift to receive the priceless gift,
Which the Christ-child brings to bless them,
With His love and life and light.

SPIRIT OF BROTHERHOOD—America, the truth has been given to thee. There is no name but His name to set all men free. Education is not enough; culture is not enough; wealth is not enough; Americanization is not enough. The world must be reconstructed around the cross of Christ. His teachings, and only His, can set free the multitude of races and peoples who have sought freedom from thee. His light is the only light that can illumine the nations that sit in darkness. The hour of thy opportunity strikes.

LIBERTY [*stepping forward*]—Men call me Liberty. They have followed me through peril, pain and death. I am the vision beautiful which has lured them to America, yet I am a phantom which leads man to destruction save for this [*throws back cape and holds up the cross*]. There is no liberty, but the liberty wherewith Christ has made men free. Henceforth, let America and all the world know me as *Christian* Liberty.

IMMIGRANT [*faces America, recites, or sings to tune, "America the Beautiful"*]—

"Our cries, our prayers ascend to God.
　Men stifle them for gain.
O promised land, O blood-bought sod,
　Let us not call in vain.
　　America! America!
A bright star lured to thee,
　It beckoned us, adventurous,
The star of liberty.

"Although thy churches rise on high,
　With spires of iron and steel,
They can not bring the Saviour nigh
　Unless our woes you feel.
　　America! America!
We ask this boon of thee,
　To lives adrift, the priceless gift
Of Christian liberty.

"For only Christ can set men free
　And give them vision new;
Grant us our fairest dream to see,
　O land where dreams come true.
　　America! America!
O dream of brotherhood,
　Marching abreast, no man oppressed,
All eyes upraised to God."

AMERICA—

"Now have I gathered me glory and power,
Strength for the coming of destiny's hour:
Artisans toiling with brain and with hands,
Money kings issuing magic commands,
Factories stirring with fertile unrest,

20

Acres with cattle and sugar cane blest,
Yet I have blinded mine eyes to the need,
Lured by the temptings of comfort and greed.
Children have languished and mothers have mourned,
Labor has sought me with cries I have scorned.
Now, challenged by gifts of honor and power,
Over the earth I hear striking the hour!"

LIBERTY [*offering cross to America*]—

"Lift up the cross, the world's desire,
That all mankind may see,
Till heavenward mounts the torch's fire
Of Christian liberty.
America! America!
Lift up the cross of Christ,
Through gain and loss, lift up the cross,
Lift up the cross of Christ."

SPIRIT OF BROTHERHOOD [*while all characters kneel*]—

God of the nations, hear our call;
Thou who art Father of us all,
Show us our part in Thy great plan
For the vast brotherhood of man.

May we, a nation blest with light,
Be ever truer to the right.
That nations in our life may see
The power which we derive from Thee.

Let us with earnestness of youth
Care only for pursuit of truth;
O may we feel Thy guidance still,
And heed the impulse of Thy will.

Thus, as Thy kingdom cometh here,
Shall it throughout the earth draw near;
And loyalty to country then
Shall reach out to include all men.

—*Vera Campbell.*

RECESSIONAL [*entire cast and choir sing as they depart down center or side aisles, in following order:* HERALD, TRUMPETERS, AMERICA, INDIAN, PIONEER, NEGRO, IMMIGRANT, ORIENTALS, ROME, GREECE, BABYLONIA, EGYPT, LIBERTY, JUSTICE, SPIRIT OF BROTHERHOOD *and* CHOIR]—

> My country is the world,
> My flag, with stars impearled,
>   Fills all the skies.
> All the round earth I claim,
> Peoples of every name,
> And all inspiring fame,
>   My heart would prize.
>
> Mine are all lands and seas,
> All flowers shrubs and trees,
>   All life's design.
> My heart within me thrills,
> For all uplifted hills,
> And for all streams and rills,
>   The world is mine.
>
> And all men are my kin,
> Since every man hath been
>   Blood of my blood.
> I glory in the grace
> And strength of every race,
> And joy in every trace
>   Of brotherhood.

—*Robert Whittaker, in "The Baptist."*

Mothers of Men

A PAGEANT FOR MOTHER'S DAY

CHARACTERS

MODERN MOTHER.
MODERN FATHER.
THE GIRL (aged fifteen).
THE BOY (aged seventeen).
INDIAN MOTHER (with papoose).
PILGRIM MOTHER (with baby or small child).
COLONIAL MOTHER (with son or daughter).
PIONEER MOTHER (with two small children).
SLAVE MOTHER (with small child).
CIVIL WAR MOTHER (with soldier son).
WIDOWED MOTHER (with several children).
WORLD WAR MOTHER (with soldier son).
IMMIGRANT MOTHERS (with children).
COMMUNITY MOTHER (with children).

COSTUMES

MODERN FAMILY.

Costumes of the season.

INDIAN.

Plain dress, with beads. Glossy black hair, braided.

PILGRIM.

Plain dress of gray, with white kerchief and cap.

COLONIAL.

Costume of the period; white hair.

23

PIONEER.

Plain dress, with shawl and bonnet.

SLAVE.

Plain dress, with red kerchief or small shawl on head.

CIVIL WAR MOTHER.

Costume typical of that period.

WIDOW.

Plain dress of black or dark blue.

WORLD WAR MOTHER.

Costume typical of that period.

IMMIGRANTS.

Costumes of Italy, Germany, Poland, Austria, etc.

COMMUNITY MOTHER.

Modern afternoon dress.

ARRANGEMENT

The platform is arranged to represent a living-room, with reading table at right, and davenport or piano at left. In addition to chairs for the family, there should be ten comfortable chairs for the various MOTHERS. The scene opens with MODERN FATHER, MOTHER and the GIRL seated around reading table.

PAGEANT

CHOIR—"Motherhood, the Beautiful." [*Tune, "Materna," by Alice C. Hoffman.*]

Oh, beautiful for loving care, for sacrificing deeds,
For self-forgetfulness so rare, that tends to all our needs;
O Motherhood! O Motherhood! God shed His grace on thee,
And crown thy good, O Motherhood! from sea to shining sea.

Oh, beautiful for tireless feet, whose patient, loving stress
A thoroughfare for childhood beat across life's wilderness;
O Motherhood! O Motherhood! we find in thee no flaw,
We find there but a kingdom fair where love is more than law.

Oh, beautiful for vision rare, that sees beyond our faults,
And with a wealth of loving care our baser self exalts;
O Motherhood! O Motherhood! God shed His grace on thee,
And crown thy good, O Motherhood, from sea to shining sea.

GIRL—I wonder where Brother went this evening.

FATHER—I sent him to the market to get some provisions for tomorrow. He should be returning soon.

MOTHER—I think I hear him coming now.

BOY [*entering with packages and bouquet, which he places on table*]—There, Dad, I guess I got everything.

MOTHER—Oh, aren't these flowers lovely! I'll get a vase. [*Exits.*]

BOY—Those are the best I could find at this hour, Dad. [*Sits and reads.*]

FATHER—I think they'll do very nicely, Son. [MOTHER *returns with vase and arranges flowers.*]

GIRL—Why the extravagance of the flowers, Daddy?

FATHER—They are for Mother's Day tomorrow. Every one is supposed to wear a white blossom in memory of a mother who has gone, and a colored blossom in honor of a living mother.

GIRL—When and where and how did that idea get started, I wonder.

FATHER [*with notes in his magazine*]—The idea was that of Miss Anna Jarvis, of Philadelphia, when she was requested by a Virginia Sunday-school superintendent to arrange a memorial service for her deceased mother, who had been a moving spirit in the community. She states that the vision for a wider observance of such a service for all mothers, with a day set apart for it, came to her when she considered the lack of consideration for absent and departed mothers among worldly-minded, busy grown-ups. The idea grew as popular sentiment was awakened, state after state adopting the plan, and finally, during the Presidency of Woodrow Wilson it became a national holiday.

GIRL—It is a beautiful custom, isn't it?

MOTHER—Indeed it is, my girl, and it is easy to honor the mothers who are with us, but we seldom stop to pay tribute to the mothers of yesterday, who have helped to build our nation, and who are the mothers of men in days gone by. The pages of American history are filled with the brave deeds of those mothers. All of the ideals which have made our country great are built upon the foundations laid by the motherhood of America. As a nation we might well say with Abraham Lincoln, "All that we are and all that we ever shall be, we owe to the mothers of America." If you will bring me your history, I will show you some of these mothers.

GIRL [*gives book to* MOTHER *and sits by her side on a low stool*]—Oh, that will be splendid. Wouldn't it be great if some of them should come to life?

MOTHER—Perhaps we *will* see them in a new light. See, here in the very first chapter is the picture of an Indian mother. [INDIAN MOTHER *enters with papoose on back, paces back and forth, then sits.*] She is a *real* American, for she was here before the white man ever came. She loved her baby, as do women of all races, and she was obedient and faithful to the servitude which the men placed upon her. And the Indian mother of today is just as devoted and loyal.

CHOIR—"God Bless Our Native Land." [*Two verses.*]

MOTHER—The first white mother in America, of course, was the Pilgrim mother. [PILGRIM MOTHER *enters with baby in arms, paces during narrative, then sits.*] Driven here by religious persecutions, she desired that her children should be free to worship God as they pleased, and as she should lead them to the Light. Through days of danger, starvation and hardship her faith never wavered. With freedom to study the open Bible, her only guide, she built up an unfaltering faith in God which has been one of America's richest heritages.

CHOIR—"O God, Beneath Thy Guiding Hand." [*One verse.*]

MOTHER—When the first states were established and later formed into a union or federation known as the Colonies, the mothers continued the steadfast faith and loyalty laid down by their grandmothers and great-grandmothers. [COLONIAL MOTHER *enters with babe or small child, paces during narrative, then sits.*] With her heart burning for the cause of liberty, the Colonial mother gave of both her sons and her daughters to serve our country, while she herself served steadfastly at home, or donned a uniform and served in the ranks. The Colonial mother thus put upon the altar of liberty all she possessed, and gave us an example of courage and of faith in God which has been our heritage through the centuries.

CHOIR—"Jesus, Saviour, Pilot Me." [*One verse.*]

MOTHER—With the development and expansion of our country through the West, thousands of mothers went unflinchingly over untrod hills and vales, by the side of their husbands and with their little families, to explore the great unknown. [PIONEER MOTHER, *leading one or two small children, enters, paces a bit, then sits.*] These pioneer mothers, filled with the spirit of adventure, were often called upon to use the gun, wield the ax, drive the nails and sometimes dig the grave for their loved ones. But these burdens did not take away her ideals of home, school and church. We owe her much for the lesson that honest toil is honorable.

CHOIR—"Lead, Kindly Light." [*One or two verses.*]

MOTHER—Early in the nineteenth century slavery was introduced into our fair land and then trouble began—trouble for our nation as well as trouble for the blacks and the whites. [NEGRO MOTHER *enters, leading small child.*] These slave mothers loved their children and there were many sad separations when they were sold at auction. Choking their sorrow and obedient under the lash, these poor women gave us a lesson of unusual devotion. Always religious, they found great comfort in singing their spirituals.

CHOIR—"Nobody Knows the Trouble I'se Seen."

MOTHER—Then came those terrible days when our country was torn by civil strife. [*Enter* CIVIL WAR MOTHER *with soldier son; they have a fond embrace and he departs, the* MOTHER *waving cheerfully, then sitting sadly.*] The Civil War mothers of both the North and the South were called upon to give their sons for the cause which both believed was right. During four years and longer they lived with heavy and anxious hearts, and thereby have given us again the lesson of sacrifice handed down from Pilgrim ancestors.

CHOIR—"Just Before the Battle, Mother." [*One verse.*]

MOTHER—Throughout all the years of American history there are thousands of unrecorded heroines among the mothers who have been bereft of their husbands. [WIDOW *with several children enters; she sits and they kneel beside her.*] These noble women, by the grace of God, spared the torture of their Oriental sisters, are unequaled examples of bravery and devotion. These saddened homes often are the result of the intemperance and crime which prevails throughout our land, and therefore should be a challenge to every Christian to help remove such evils and the attendant sorrow.

CHOIR—"His Eye Is on the Sparrow." [*One verse.*]

Mothers of Men

MOTHER—As we continue to turn the pages of history we come to the record of those stirring days when our country reached her hands across the seas to help make the world safe for democracy. [WORLD WAR MOTHER *and son in khaki enter, have a fond embrace and he departs, the* MOTHER *waving cheerfully, then sitting sadly.*] American mothers by the thousand, from all stations in life, gave their sons to the greatest conflict which the world has ever known. Fresh in the memory of many today is the sacrifice of these gold-star mothers who were loyal to the heritage which they received from their sisters of the past.

CHOIR—"Keep the Home Fires Burning." [*One verse.*]

MOTHER—Scattered abroad through our country and in every state, we find the immigrant mothers, who have had a strong influence upon our national life. [IMMIGRANT MOTH-ERS, *women of several European nationalities, enter, accompanied by children, and sit in groups.*] These brave women left their native lands in search of greater freedom, both of worship and of service, and have given their sons and their daughters to our country as musicians, authors, doctors, lawyers, merchants, scientists, engineers, miners and general laborers. They, too, have received the heritage of love and sacrifice which they are passing on to us. Let us hear one of their national sacred hymns.

CHOIR—"Christ for the World We Sing."

MOTHER—Here we are at the last chapter in your history and we behold a glorious picture of the mothers of today. [COMMUNITY MOTHER *enters with several children, and sit in a class group.*] Modern inventions have equipped many homes with labor-saving devices, so that women have more time for study, recreation and service. They work in the numerous community organizations and in the various departments of the church, and are striving constantly to make the world a better and more beautiful place.

CHOIR—"Lord, Speak to Me, that I May Speak." [*Two verses.*]

GIRL—Those were glorious pictures, Mother mine, but there should be at least one more, to present mothers like your own dear self—the home mother—who thinks of her family first of all in these times of stress and lawlessness, plans and prepares our meals, mends our clothes, studies with us, plays with us, and trains us in the ways of righteousness. Yours is the example of sacrifice and devotion which I must foster in the years to come, so that women of the future may be loyal to their heritage and be real mothers of men.

[*During the closing hymn the* FATHER, *the* GIRL *and the* BOY *gather around the* MOTHER *in center of platform, with other* MOTHERS *at rear and sides.*]

CHOIR—"Faith of Our Mothers." [*Author unknown.*]

Faith of our mothers, living yet,
　　In cradle song and bedtime prayer,
In nursery lore and fireside love,
　　Thy presence still pervades the air:
Faith of our mothers, living faith,
　　We will be true to thee till death.

Faith of our mothers, lavish faith,
　　The fount of childhood's trust and grace;
Oh, may thy consecration prove
　　The well-spring of a nobler race:
Faith of our mothers, lavish faith,
　　We will be true to thee till death.

Faith of our mothers, guiding faith,
　　For youthful longing—youthful doubt;
How blurred our vision, blind our way,
　　Thy providential care without:
Faith of our mothers, guiding faith,
　　We will be true to thee till death.

Mothers of Men

Faith of our mothers, Christian faith,
  In truth beyond our man-made creeds,
Still serve the home and save the church,
  And breathe thy spirit through our deeds:
Faith of our mothers, Christian faith,
  We will be true to thee till death.

One Father of All*

CHARACTERS

COSTUMES

READER.

May wear modern clothes or an Oriental robe.

PARSEES.

Long, white gowns with veils covering head and entire face, except eyes. One carries an earthen bowl containing a short, lighted candle. All wear many beads and bracelets.

FETISH WORSHIPERS.

Long robes of dark red or brown, with adornments of heavy beads and strings of small objects around neck, large earrings,

---

* Adapted from a worship service prepared by Pearl Forsyth and Martha Race. Published by the Woman's Press, New York, and used by permission.

3   33

armlets, and headbands of feathers. Faces painted grotesquely with chalk of various colors. One worshiper carries the image of an ugly god.

BUDDHISTS.

The boy represents a priest and wears a yellow robe, with a skull cap (or coil of red or black cloth) and gray beard. One girl represents Japan and wears a bright kimono with a wide girdle which is tied into a large, flat bow on back, and has pom-poms in hair, the latter being glossy black. One represents Korea and wears a high-waisted skirt of light color and a jacket of contrasting color. One represents Burma and wears a skirt of stripes running horizontally, with a jacket of contrasting color, and ornaments in her hair, which also is black. Each girl has a lighted candle and vase of flowers.

CONFUCIANISTS.

Pajamas of plain color (preferably blue) and sleeveless jackets or vests of black cloth. Wide-brimmed straw hats, such as are worn on the farm. One brings a black paper banner, about 8 x 24 inches, on which is a smaller strip of red with several Chinese characters made with black crayon. The other worshiper has a small metal vase or tin can containing three lighted joss-sticks, or punk, and a bowl with a Chinese lily.

HINDUS.

Flowing robes of bright colors, with head scarfs, one end of latter crossed under chin and thrown over shoulder. Each has a small bowl, supposed to contain offerings of rice, flour and spices. All wear many beads and bracelets.

MOHAMMEDANS.

Long gowns of dark colors and turbans of bright cloth. Veil of black lace or net across nose and tied at back of head, thus covering the mouth and reaching to chest. Two of the worshipers have small prayer rugs.

PHARISEE AND PUBLICAN.

PHARISEE has an elaborate embroidered robe, and the PUBLICAN a simple tunic, each with a head scarf.

The Church.

> Long, white robe with veil arranged in the manner of the Red
> Cross workers (low on forehead and hair concealed). She may
> have adornments of gold beads and bracelets.

ARRANGEMENT

Special scenery is not needed, but draperies will add greatly to the
effect. The only illumination comes from several groups of candle tapers
and two floor lamps, one of the latter being placed by the piano at left
and one for the READER at right. Several footlights or one large flood-
light also necessary. Entrances are at right and left. A soft musical
accompaniment may be used throughout, especially during entrance of
each group. The latter worship in center of platform and then retire to
the sides, where places have been assigned, forming a semicircle at the
close. Players should strive to convey a feeling of deep, unsatisfied longing
for spiritual satisfaction.

ACTION

Fetish Worshipers.

> Both enter together, one having the image of an ugly god, which
> is placed upon the altar; then both worshipers kneel and bow head
> and arms to floor three times, repeating with each prostration,
> "Hear, O God! Send rain!" Then they kneel upright and repeat
> the prayer three times, rapidly, clapping hands, and then retire
> to sides. A tom-tom may be heard behind scenes.

Parsees.

> One girl bears in her uplifted hands the bowl with candle flame,
> and stands in center. The others stand right and left, facing her.
> Raising their arms toward the flame, they sink slowly to their knees,
> while READER chants the prayer, then retire.

Buddhists.

> The priest enters first, places an image of Buddha on the altar,
> kneels a moment before it, then stands behind it. The three girls
> enter and sit on floor, facing altar, listening to the prayer of the
> priest and the voice of the READER. Then they arise and place
> candles and vases on the altar.

35

CONFUCIANISTS.

> One pins his banner on the altar and the other places his lily and
> joss-sticks upon the altar. Both kneel, place hands upon the floor
> and bow reverently three times, while READER prays.

HINDUS.

> The three girls enter and place offerings upon altar. One stands
> in center, elevates arms level with shoulders, bends elbows, fore-
> arms at right angles to upper arms, palms outward. She turns
> slowly around, keeping feet on same spot. The others kneel with
> hands upon the floor, faces six or eight inches from floor. The
> one in center comes to a standstill, and, while cymbals are heard
> behind scenes, the READER intones.

MOHAMMEDANS.

> Follow the action described in manuscript.

PHARISEE AND PUBLICAN.

> Follow action described in manuscript.

PAGEANT

HYMNS [*suggested*]—"O Worship the King," "Ancient
of Days," "Jesus Saves."

PRAYER [*by minister*].

PRAYER HYMN [*suggested*]—"Love Divine," "Ancient of
Days."

OFFERING AND ANNOUNCEMENT OF PAGEANT.

READER—Listen to the words of Isaiah, the prophet:

"Hast thou not known? hast thou not heard? The ever-
lasting God, Jehovah, the Creator of the ends of the earth,
fainteth not, neither is weary; there is no searching of his
understanding. He giveth power to the faint; and to him
who hath no might he increaseth strength. Even the youths
shall faint and be weary, and the young men shall utterly
fall, but they that wait for Jehovah shall renew their strength:

they shall mount up with wings as eagles; they shall run and not be weary; they shall walk, and not faint."

And the prophet Micah has also written:

"Wherewith shall I come before Jehovah, and bow myself before the high God? shall I come before him with burnt-offerings, with calves a year old? will Jehovah be pleased with thousands of rams, or with ten thousand rivers of oil? Shall I give my first-born for my transgression, the fruit of my body for the sin of my soul? He hath showed thee, O man, what is good; and what doth Jehovah require of thee, but to do justly, and to love kindness, and to walk humbly with thy God?"

[*Music.*]

READER—The *Persian Parsees* come to worship. [*Three girls enter and perform.*]

That I shall ask of thee, tell it me right, O Ormazd.
Who created the lights of good effect and the darkness?
Who created the sleep of good effect and the activities?
Who created morning, noon and night, reminding the priest always of his duties?

That I shall ask of thee, tell it me right, O Ormazd.
What guardian angel may tell me good things to perform five times a day,
The duties enjoined by thyself, O Ormazd,
And to recite those prayers which are communicated for the welfare of all things by the Good Mind?

Whatever good intended for the increase of life is to be had, may it come to me.
Standing by thy fire, among the worshipers who pray to thee,
I will be mindful of righteousness as long as I shall be able.
I believe thee to be the best Being of all, the Source of light for all the world.

[*Music.*]

READER—*African Fetish Worshipers* make their petitions.

[*Music.*]

READER—The *Buddhists of Japan, Korea and Burma* come to their temple.

BUDDHIST PRIEST—

Lord Buddha, in earth and heaven and hell incomparable.
All-honored, wisest, best, most pitiful;
The teacher of Nirvana and the Law.

READER [*representing voices of women worshipers*]—

O thou eternal One, thou perfection of Time,
Thou truest Truth, thou immutable Essence of all change,
Thou most excellent Radiance of mercy,
Thou infinite Compassion, thou Pity, thou Charity,
I take my refuge in thy name and thee;
I take my refuge in thy law of good;
I take my refuge in thy order.

[*Music.*]

READER—The *Confucianists* come to worship their god. [*With high nasal tone:*]

Confucius, Confucius, how great was Confucius!
Before him there was no Confucius.
Since him there has been no other.
Confucius, Confucius, how great was Confucius!

[*Music.*]

READER—The *Hindus* come to worship their gods. [*After they make their petitions the* READER *says:*]

The embodied spirit has a thousand heads,
A thousand feet, a thousand eyes,
Around on every side, enveloping the earth,
Yet filling space no larger than a span.
He is himself this very universe.
He is whatever is, has been and shall be;
He is the lord of immortality.

All creatures are one-fourth of him;
Three-fourths are of that which is immortal in the sky,
Of Siva, Vishnu, Brahma; each may be
First, second, third, among the blessed three.

[*Music.*]

READER—The *Mohammedans* come to prayer. [*One enters and stands at center.*]

One silver crescent in the twilight sky is hanging,
Another tips the dome of yonder solemn mosque,
And now the muezzin's call is heard, sonorous, clanging,
Through thronged bazaar, concealed harem and cool ki-cak.

[*A bell or gong is heard.*]

In the prophet's name, God is God, and there is no other.

MOHAMMEDAN—

Come to prayer, come to security.
Allah is most great. There is no deity but Allah.

[*Two others enter with rugs and kneel.*]
READER—

On roofs, in streets or closet, each beside his brother,
Each Moslem kneels, his forehead turned toward Mecca's shrine.
And all the world forgotten in the one thought divine.

TWO MOHAMMEDANS—Allah is great. There is no God but Allah.

[*Music.*]

READER—The *Pharisee* and *Publican* enter.

PHARISEE [*standing at right*]—"God, I thank thee that I am not as other men are, extortioners, unjust, adulterers, or even as this publican."

PUBLICAN [*kneeling at left*]—"God, be merciful to me, a sinner."

[*Music.*]

READER—The *Spirit of the Church* enters.

[READER *retires.*]

CHOIR—"The Church's One Foundation" [*one verse*], or "Take Time To Be Holy."

CHURCH—Have we not all one Father? Hath not one God created us?

[PUBLICAN *kneels at end of semicircle.*]

CHURCH—Why do we deal treacherously, every man against his brother, profaning the covenant of our fathers?

[PHARISEE *kneels at opposite end.*]

CHURCH—But be not ye called rabbi, for One is your Father, and all ye are brethren.

[PERSIAN *kneels beside* PUBLICAN.]

CHURCH—And call no man your Father on the earth, for One is your Father, even He who is in heaven.

[AFRICAN *kneels beside* PHARISEE.]

CHURCH—We know that we have passed out of death into life, because we love the brethren.

[BUDDHIST *kneels beside* PERSIAN.]

CHURCH—Mother and brethren are these that hear the Word of God and do it.

[JAPANESE *kneels beside* BUDDHIST. KOREAN *and* BURMESE *kneel beside* AFRICAN.]

GROUP—Lord, teach us to pray.

CHURCH—In praying, use not vain repetitions as the heathen do, for they think that they shall be heard for their much speaking.

GROUP—"Our Father who art in heaven."

PIANO—"Holy, Holy, Holy!"

CHURCH—We bow our knees unto the Father, from whom every family in heaven and on earth is named.

GROUP—"Hallowed be thy name."

PIANO—"Come, Thou Almighty King."

CHURCH—"Let every one that nameth the name of the Lord depart from unrighteousness. Be ye transformed by the renewing of your mind, that ye may prove what is the good and acceptable and perfect will of God." The time is fulfilled and the kingdom of God is at hand. Repent ye.

"They shall come from the east and the west, and from the north and the south, and shall sit down in the kingdom of God, and behold, there are last who shall be first, and there are first who shall be last."

GROUP—"Thy kingdom come."

PIANO—"Jesus Shall Reign."

CHURCH—"I have been crucified with Christ and it is no longer I that live, but Christ who liveth in me.

"Even so reckon ye also, yourselves, to be dead unto sin, but alive unto God in Christ Jesus.

"Let not sin therefore reign in your mortal body, that ye should obey the lusts thereof: neither present your members unto sin, as instruments of unrighteousness; but present yourselves unto God, as alive from the dead, and your members as instruments of righteousness unto God."

GROUP—"Thy will be done on earth as it is in heaven."

PIANO—"Take My Life and Let It Be."

CHURCH—"Be not therefore anxious, saying, What shall we eat? or what shall we drink? or wherewithal shall we be clothed?"

GROUP—"Give us this day our daily bread."

PIANO—"Bread of Heaven" or "Break Thou the Bread of Life."

CHURCH—"Rejoice in the Lord always: again I say, Rejoice. Let your forbearance be known unto all men. The Lord is at hand.

"How oft shall my brother sin against me, and I forgive him? Until seven times? I say not unto thee, until seven times, but until seventy times seven.

"If ye forgive men their trespasses, your heavenly Father will also forgive you."

GROUP—"And forgive us our trespasses as we forgive those who trespass against us."

PIANO—"I Am Coming, Lord."

CHURCH—"For in many things we all stumble. But Christ hath said, Whoso shall cause one of these little ones that believe on me to stumble, it is better for him that a millstone should be hanged about his neck and that he should be drowned in the depths of the sea.

"For in that he himself hath suffered being tempted, he is able to help them that are tempted."

GROUP—"And lead us not into temptation, but deliver us from evil."

PIANO—"Yield Not to Temptation."

CHURCH—"The Lord hath prepared his throne in the heavens, and his kingdom ruleth over all.

"And Jesus said unto them, All power is given unto me in heaven and in earth.

"I am the Lord: that is my name: and my glory will I not give to another."

GROUP—"For thine is the kingdom, and the power, and the glory for ever."

PIANO [or CHOIR]—"Glory Be to the Father."

CHURCH—For none of us liveth unto himself.

GROUP—And none dieth to himself.

CHURCH—For whether we live,

GROUP—We live unto the Lord.

CHURCH—Or whether we die,

GROUP—We die unto the Lord.

CHURCH—Whether we live, therefore, or die,
GROUP—We are the Lord's.
CHOIR—"Dear Lord and Father of Mankind."
GROUP—[Recite the Lord's Prayer.]
[*Exit.*]
TALK BY MINISTER—"The Fatherhood of God."
SONG—"All Hail the Power of Jesus' Name."
BENEDICTION.

Just Around the Corner

A PAGEANT SHOWING NEGLECTED AREAS IN THE UNITED STATES

CHARACTERS

READERS

SPIRIT OF SERVICE   INTERPRETER

PROPHET ISAIAH

TABLEAUX

GROUP OF MODERN INDIANS

GROUP OF LUMBERMEN

FRONTIER FARMER AND FAMILY

NEGRO FAMILY

MEXICAN FAMILY

THREE CHINESE LAUNDRYMEN

MORMON MISSIONARY

GROUP OF AMERICAN CITIZENS

JEWISH MERCHANT

GROUP OF IMMIGRANTS

INSPECTOR

MOUNTAIN FAMILY

COSTUMES

SPIRIT OF SERVICE.

Modern dress or flowing robe. Reads from book.

ISAIAH.

Tunic reaching to shoe tops, with cloak of striped cloth. Turban of bright cloth, bound with cord. Bare legs with sandals. Dark beard. Reads from scroll.

THE INTERPRETER.

Modern dress. Reads from Bible notes.

TABLEAU CHARACTERS.

These costumes are either suggested in the scene setting or will be found in section of "National Costumes."

ARRANGEMENTS

Careful advance preparation should be made for the scenery, which at first thought may seem quite difficult, is very easily arranged, and with several stage hands it can be quickly placed while choir sings. The house fronts used in several scenes may be painted with chalk on wallboard and braced into position with props in the rear. Small trees are prepared to stand upright like Christmas trees.

If special scenery is not available, folding screens may be used on each side of the platform, with door effects for entrances. One curtain in front is necessary.

The tableau characters may appear motionless, as painted pictures, or may move about in silent pantomime.

PAGEANT

ORGAN AND CHOIR PRELUDE—"The Red, White and Blue."

SERVICE [*standing at center, outside curtain*]—Missionaries have been at work in this country ever since John Eliot worked among the red men surrounding the first Pilgrim settlements, and they have been the highway builders of schools, industries, hospitals, playgrounds, social settlements, colleges and universities, as well as the great chain of churches which they have organized across the continent. For more than a century the work has been promoted by numerous home mission boards of several denominations, but even now we are only half awake to the great need, and there are today vast areas of our country which are quite destitute of Christian work and quite as heathen as the heart of Africa.

Nearly 2,700 years ago the prophet Isaiah revealed the glory of the new Zion unto the people. Let us hear his word and its interpretation for us.

[ISAIAH *and* INTERPRETER *enter and stand at right and left of platform, outside curtain. They exit after dialogue.*]

ISAIAH—"The wilderness and the solitary place shall be glad for the judgments of the Lord; and the desert shall rejoice and blossom as the rose."

INTERPRETER—There are wildernesses and deserts in the midst of the most fertile regions. They are spiritual wildernesses and deserts of the soul, and they are far more terrible than the deserts of sand and the wildernesses of the forests. What are we, the farmers of the Lord, doing to cultivate these waste places?

ISAIAH—"It shall blossom abundantly, and rejoice even with joy and singing: the glory of Lebanon shall be given unto it, the excellency of Carmel and Sharon, they shall see the glory of the Lord, and the excellency of our God."

INTERPRETER—Out of the desert places of the nation have come some of the noblest men and women of our national history. Abraham Lincoln came from such a desert place.

ISAIAH—"Strengthen ye the weak hands and confirm the feeble knees."

INTERPRETER—The people who live in the neglected places are often weak and feeble, but what can we expect? What would we be, mentally or spiritually, without the mind food and the soul food which have been provided for us so abundantly and freely all our lives?

ISAIAH—"Say to them that are of a fearful heart, Be strong, fear not: behold, your God will come with vengeance, even God with a recompense; he will come and save you."

INTERPRETER—God is eager to go to these neglected parts of our land, but how can He go unless we go? We have this fearful responsibility, that by our selfishness and indifference we can actually thwart God.

ISAIAH—"Then the eyes of the blind shall be opened and the ears of the deaf shall be unstopped."

INTERPRETER—The people who live in these underprivileged places are deaf to the angel voices that fill our heavens, and blind to the vision of heavenly glory which fills our eyes. Christ is ready and glad to work two miracles for their sakes.

ISAIAH—"Then shall the lame man leap as an hart, and the tongue of the dumb sing: for in the wilderness shall waters break out, and streams in the desert."

INTERPRETER—Missionary work in these neglected areas is as refreshing as streams in a desert. We are so familiar with church work and church influences that we can not realize how delightful and novel it is to those who are not privileged to enjoy it regularly and often.

ISAIAH—"And the parched ground shall become a pool, and the thirsty land springs of water: in the habitation of dragons, where each lay, shall be grass with reeds and rushes."

INTERPRETER—The neglected areas are full of wild beasts. We may neglect those places, but Satan does not neglect them. Sin is there if the gospel is not there. We are poor strategists; we allow the enemy to take possession of our ground.

ISAIAH—"And an highway shall be there, and a way, and it shall be called the way of holiness; the unclean shall not pass over it; but it shall be for those: the wayfaring men, though fools, shall not err therein."

INTERPRETER—John the Baptist came to prepare the way of the Lord, and that is a part of the task of every Christian.

How much John-the-Baptist work have we done? In what condition are the roads that Jesus would like to tread?

CHOIR—"God Bless Our Native Land."

SERVICE—Many of the neglected areas in our country are surrounded by vigorous and prosperous Christian communities, which move along serenely, unconscious of the paganism just around the corner. The slums of any large city need Christian work as much as China needs it, but what are we doing about it? Whether these neglected folk are just around the corner or on the other side of the continent, we are responsible for them in proportion to our ability to help them, since this is one country and we are all citizens of the whole land. Tonight we are to visualize some of these neglected fields and strive to arouse ourselves to our great responsibility. But first let us look to God in prayer, while we sing. [*Steps to right of platform.*]

CHOIR [*tune, "Am I a Soldier of the Cross?"*]—

> Teach us, O Lord, true brotherhood
> In daily thought and deed,
> That we may tread with humble heart
> The path where Thou dost lead.
>
> Give us the courage, Lord, to fight
> With Thee all greed of gold;
> To fight until Thy kingdom's won,
> Thy kingdom long foretold.
>
> Love then shall reign supreme o'er all,
> O'er heart and mind and hand,
> Eternal love and brotherhood
> In all this storm-tossed land.
>
> With vision clear and steadfast heart
> So let us follow Thee,
> E'en though it be that weary road
> Which leads to Calvary.

SCENE 1

[*Outdoor setting, with trees, tepee and camp fire.* GROUP OF ADULT INDIANS *grinding corn, weaving baskets and blankets, and molding pottery.* INDIAN CHILDREN *playing. The costumes should be of the modern Indian type, as described in section of "National Costumes."*]

SERVICE [*during tableau*]—There are about 350,000 Indians in the United States, and our Government is aiming to make them American citizens as fast as possible. It is dividing their lands among them and getting them to take up the rights and the duties of citizens. It has actually accomplished more than half of this gigantic task. Now the work of the church ought to go on at least as fast as the work of the state, but it does not. The Indian should be Christianized at least as fast as he is adopted into the citizenry of the nation, but this is not being accomplished. As yet only one-fourth of the Indian tribes have ever heard of Jesus. The Indians make noble Christians. Should we not help to plant their feet on the new trail?

CURTAIN

CHOIR—"Jesus Saves."

SCENE 2

[*Outdoor setting, with trees banked in rear. Front of a bunk house may be seen at right, and a pile of wood at left. Axes and saws leaning against house and trees.* GROUP OF LUMBERMEN, *in coarse clothes of woodsmen style, lounging around.*]

SERVICE [*during tableau*]—About half a million men are engaged in cutting timber and transporting the logs to sawmills. At least 200,000 of these men work in the forests of the Northern Pacific Coast, and the others are scattered in many states. The labor in these lumber camps is migratory, but in recent years the men have been cared for with a considerable degree of comfort, the food being first-class and served in great abundance. These laborers are radically-minded and are in sad need of Christian ministrations. The self-sacrificing labors of Frank Higgins called attention to the religious destitution of the woodsmen and to the fine response which they give to Christian work. The men are rough and poor, many vices get hold of them, but they are strong and manly and very appreciative of anything that is done for them. The work is full of hardships and the laborers are very few.

CURTAIN

CHOIR—"Send the Light."

SCENE 3

[*Outdoor setting, with shocks of wheat or corn in background. Front of shack used in Scene 2. A tiny porch may be added and covered with paper vines. Rain-water barrel at one side of porch, and bench on opposite side. Washing hanging on a line.* FRONTIER FARMER AND FAMILY *in farm clothes; the man working with a farm tool; the woman washing at a tub on bench; older girl peeling potatoes; older boy drawing water from a well at one side, and small children playing.*]

SERVICE [*during tableau*]—Many farming regions are neglected areas, though they may be near large cities. But if no regular religious services are available, they are as much neglected as if they lived hundreds of miles away. There is a county in a Western state whose area is more than five thousand square miles, and religious work is carried on at only four or five points. The county has twenty-four school districts, and in only three of these is any kind of religious work carried on. Another county of 4,600 square miles has religious work in only three of the eighteen school districts. Such are the conditions in many areas of the West, and millions of people are living on such frontiers. They are hungry for the gospel and look upon the rare missionary as an angel from heaven. Is it not a shame that so few missionaries go out to them?

CURTAIN

CHOIR—"Speed Away."

SCENE 4

[*Outdoor setting, with shack used in Scene 3, and background of trees.* NEGRO FAMILY: *Negro woman is washing at tub, with a red bandanna kerchief tied around her head. A Negro man is splitting wood. Children playing.*]

SERVICE [*during tableau*]—About every ninth person in the United States is a Negro. The race in America is increasing much faster than our Christian work for it is increasing. The South is doing more for the Negro than ever before, and the Negroes are doing far more for themselves than they have ever been able to do, but still the religious destitution among them is deplorable, and constitutes a danger spot in American civilization. When we think of the vast numbers involved and their importance in our American life, the Negroes form the largest neglected group in our country. Lack of education brings poverty, dependence, nonemployment, poor health and poor home conditions to the Negro, as it does to any family. Four hundred thousand Negro boys and girls, many of whom live in rural areas, have no school advantages. The Negro is naturally religious, and he throws himself with delightful fervor into its services. Let us help them enjoy this blessed privilege.

CURTAIN

Choir—"Steal Away to Jesus" [*or other Negro spiritual*].

SCENE 5

[*Courtyard of a Mexican home. Wall of house at rear made to represent concrete. Doorway in center, over which is a striped awning extending full length of the wall. Under this, at one side, is a hammock. Palms at each side of porch. Water jars at right and left.* Mexican Family: *Men and women in Mexican costumes; have guitars and tambourines.*]

Service [*during tableau*]—We have many thousands of Mexicans in the Southwest. They have come to us from the old Mexican ownership of those states. If we look at the Mexican towns just across the border line and compare them with the United States towns immediately to the north, the contrast is like journeying a thousand miles. The Mexicans in our country respond to the work of the missionaries and of the mission schools whenever they have a chance. They become faithful Christians and often produce honored ministers of the gospel. But the Mexicans are terribly neglected and few work among them. History shows that we owe a heavy debt to these people. When will the churches pay it?

CURTAIN

Choir—"O Zion, Haste."

SCENE 6

[*Arrange platform as a Chinese laundry, with shelves in rear on which packages are placed, and counter at front. Charts with Chinese characters on wall.* Three Chinese Laundrymen *are ironing at one side.*]

Service [*during tableau*]—Thousands of Hindus are in this country, more than 110,000 Japanese, more than 60,000

Chinese, and about 3,000 Koreans. Very little Christian work is done among them all. It is said that not 10 per cent of the Orientals in Oregon have ever heard the gospel. California has twenty-seven counties that average two hundred Orientals in each, and very little religious work is done for them. In the East also these people are allowed to go their way with almost no attention from the churches. We seem to have forgotten that Christianity is an Oriental religion, with a message at least as likely to win an Oriental as an Occidental. Recent developments in educational circles in China have shown that native leadership is being sought and demanded. It is a challenge and an opportunity for the Christian Chinese language schools to equip these future leaders with Christian ideals. They in turn can interpret them to those in China who need to know of the beauty and power of Christ. This is one of our responsibilities.

CURTAIN

CHOIR—"Christ for the World We Sing."

SCENE 7

[*Room where a* MORMON MISSIONARY *is talking to a* GROUP OF AMERICAN CITIZENS.]

SERVICE [*during tableau*]—Mormonism is a growing national menace and has rightly been called the "Islam of America." It controls the politics of several northwestern states, in addition to Utah. It reaches out its long tentacles over the entire nation, sending crafty missionaries to all of our great cities, to our colleges and to many small towns and villages. It holds its victims, especially the poor women, in a thrall that is worse than African slavery. In Utah there are very few Christian missionaries compared with the appalling need. Seven counties with a combined population of more than twenty thousand have no Christian work whatever. If we do not want to see our nation corrupted through and through with this cancer, we must cease to neglect its breeding place.

CURTAIN

CHOIR—"How Firm a Foundation."

SCENE 8

[*A neighborhood store, with merchandise on the shelves and counter.* JEWISH MERCHANT *stands behind counter, with several customers* (AMERICAN CITIZENS) *in front.*]

SERVICE [*during tableau*]—There are thousands of Jews in our country, and New York City is the largest Jewish settlement in the world. The Jews are very prominent in American life—in finance, in trade, in manufacturing, in literature, music and the arts. Moreover, we owe to the Jews not only the Old Testament, but the New, and our Lord Himself was a Jew. Is it not amazing that almost no Christian work is done for and with the Jews, and that they are the most neglected group of our complex American nation? Has Christianity, whose first disciples, apostles and missionaries were Jews, lost its power to hold them? Not at all. It is only that we seem to be powerless.

CURTAIN

CHOIR—"God of Our Fathers, Known of Old."

SCENE 9

[*Section of a waiting room at Ellis Island. Men, women and children* (GROUP OF IMMIGRANTS) *in costumes of European nations. Quaint telescopes, traveling bags and sacks piled about. Children playing.* INSPECTOR *at desk, making records* (*in cage enclosure, if possible*).]

55

SERVICE [*during tableau*]—It is estimated that there are in this country approximately fourteen million persons of foreign birth, plus twenty-four millions who are native-born of foreign or mixed parentage. Most of these are found in the great industrial zone east of the Mississippi and north of the Ohio Rivers. Most of the menial tasks fall to his lot; he is found in the mills, in the mines, on the highways, in foundries, in the engine and boiler rooms, and in the orchards, vineyards and gardens. These foreigners came here just as our own forefathers came, to find a better and a freer life. If we are to realize our responsibility to them, we must lay aside every prejudice. Many of them are devotedly religious, and we can help them to keep in touch with God. However, we can accomplish nothing for the foreigner until we try to sympathize with him and love him and treat him like a brother. We have before us a view of a group waiting for entrance at Ellis Island.

CURTAIN

CHOIR—"The Call of Brotherhood."

SCENE 10

[*Interior of a cabin, with fire place at rear center. Bunks in right and left corners. Rough table and chairs. Coal-oil lamp on table.* MOUNTAIN FAMILY: *Man and woman in coarse clothes are seated and smoking corncob pipes. One young lady is sewing and another is peeling potatoes. One young man is cleaning his gun and a younger one is whittling. Small children may be added, if desired.*]

SERVICE [*during tableau*]—There are two main mountain areas in the South—one east of the Mississippi and composed of the Allegheny, Cumberland and Blue Ridge Mountains; the other west of the river and known as the Ozarks. Within this area dwell about five and one-half millions of people. They are predominantly rural, the few large cities being in the valleys. In most cases each man is his own blacksmith, carpenter and cobbler. Women and girls work in the fields along with the men and boys. Agricultural conditions are being improved by county agents, schools are being improved by the states, but the churches are being sadly neglected, owing to the indifference of outside leaders. While several splendid settlements and social centers have been established by Christian influences, there is a great need for volunteer preachers and teachers in the mountain Sunday schools. Here is another opportunity to challenge every Christian.

CURTAIN

CHOIR—"Hark! the Voice of Jesus Calling."

SERVICE—"Love of God and love of country are the two noblest passions of the human heart," says Dr. Henry Van Dyke. "A man without a country is an exile in the world, and a man without God is an orphan in eternity." May the visions of service which have appeared to us tonight challenge us to go "just around the corner" and carry the Light.

SCENE 11

[*All characters facing rear wall on which American flag is hung.*]

CHOIR [*during tableau*]—"America the Beautiful."

The Lawgiver

Tableau with Song and Story

SCENES FROM THE LIFE OF MOSES

CHARACTERS

READER.
JOCHEBED_____A Hebrew Woman
MIRIAM_____Her Daughter
MOSES, AARON_____Her Sons
PHARAOH_____Ruler of Egypt
ZIBA _____His Daughter
TAPTHA, BASHAM_____Her Attendants
JETHRO_____A Priest of Midian
SON OF PHARAOH.
OFFICERS OF PHARAOH'S COURT.
AN EGYPTIAN TASKMASTER.
HEBREW SLAVES.
TWO ATTENDANTS OF PHARAOH.
FOUR DAUGHTERS OF JETHRO.
DANCING MAIDENS.
ISRAELITES.
ANGEL OF THE LORD.
TWELVE SPIES (including CALEB and JOSHUA).

COSTUMES

JOCHEBED.

Gown of dark blue, with scarf of bright red over head.

MIRIAM.

Two persons are necessary to portray this character. In Scene 2 she is a child about ten or twelve years of age, with bright dress and head scarf. In Scenes 8 and 10 she is a woman of middle age,

with costume similar to JOCHEBED's. The woman representing
JOCHEBED may also represent the older MIRIAM.

MOSES.

In Scenes 3 and 4 he is a young man with a robe of striped Egyptian cloth, reaching halfway between the knees and ankles, tied at the waist by a narrow girdle. Striped scarf tied around head, with ends hanging over ears. Sandals. In Scene 5 he has the costume of a shepherd—a tunic of tan color, made without sleeves (brown burlap will do). Has short, dark beard and carries staff. In remaining scenes he wears a long white gown, with overdrapery of dark blue, edged with red and yellow. Head turban of bright cloth. After Scene 9 he has white hair and beard, and no head covering.

AARON.

Dressed similar to MOSES, but with overdrapery of different colors. White hair and beard after Scene 9.

PHARAOH.

The young man representing the younger MOSES may take this part by adding beads, bracelets and rings. Also a cape around shoulders.

ZIBA.

This is an imaginary name given to Pharaoh's daughter. She is about sixteen or eighteen years old. Long gown of bright color, with beads and bracelets. Should have dark hair. Light veil over head.

TAPTHA AND BASHAM.

Dark-skinned women, with dresses of striped Egyptian cloth. Turbans of bright colors.

SON OF PHARAOH.

Lad of ten or twelve years, appearing only as a dead child at Pharaoh's feet. Short tunic of striped cloth.

OFFICERS.

Tunics of bright colors, reaching to knees. Capes of various colors. Bare legs with sandals or soft slippers. Dark hair and short beards. Helmet turbans made from folded gold paper.

TASKMASTER.

> Use the young man representing the younger AARON. He has a lash in one hand.

HEBREW SLAVES.

> Five will be sufficient. They wear only short pants, similar to modern athletic or track suits. They may appear in later scenes as some of the SPIES and CHILDREN OF ISRAEL by wearing a tunic, shoulder scarf and turban.

PHARAOH'S ATTENDANTS.

> Those who served for ZIBA will do. One stands on each side of him, fanning him with long-handled fans made from plumes or palm leaves.

JETHRO.

> Long white robe with overdrapery of bright cloth. Turban. White beard. The man representing the elder AARON may take this part.

JETHRO'S DAUGHTERS.

> Flowing gowns of various colors, with head scarfs of contrasting colors. The Bible mentions seven, but four will be sufficient.

DANCING MAIDENS.

> These are from the company of CHILDREN OF ISRAEL, and may include the girls representing JETHRO'S DAUGHTERS. They wear flowing robes, with beads and jewels, and also have cymbals, tambourines and harps.

CHILDREN OF ISRAEL.

> Use as many as possible, including all characters in earlier scenes.

TWELVE SPIES.

> These are selected from the CHILDREN OF ISRAEL.

ANGEL.

> Use one of the men wearing a sheet drapery, with long folds draped over arms, which are raised for "wings."

PREPARATION

Same as for pageant "Soldiers of the Cross."

SONGS AND STORIES

SCENE 1

THE OPPRESSION OF ISRAEL

CHOIR—"O for a Faith that Will Not Shrink."
READER—Ex. 1: 7-14, 22.
        Ex. 2: 1-4 (explanatory).

SCENE 2

SAVED BY A PRINCESS

CHOIR—"God Will Take Care of You."
READER—Ex. 2: 5-10.

SCENE 3

ANGERED BY SLAVERY

CHOIR—"Awake, My Soul."
READER—Ex. 2: 11-14.

SCENE 4

THE FLIGHT TO MIDIAN

CHOIR—"God of Our Fathers, Known of Old."
READER—Ex. 2: 15-21.
        Ex. 2: 23-25 (explanatory).

SCENE 5

COMMISSIONED BY GOD

CHOIR—" 'Tis by the Faith of Joys to Come."
READER—Ex. 3: 1-12, 19, 20.
        Ex. 4: 10-17, 27-31 (explanatory).

SCENE 6

THE MESSAGE TO PHARAOH

CHOIR—"There's a Wideness."
READER—Ex. 5: 1-5.
      Ex. 5: 6-19; 7: 19-25; 8; 9; 10 (explanatory).

SCENE 7

DEATH OF THE FIRST-BORN

CHOIR—"O God, Our Help in Ages Past."
READER—Ex. 11: 1-7; 12: 29-31.
      Ex. 13: 17-21; 14: 5-14, 21-23, 27-31 (explanatory).

SCENE 8

THE SONG OF THANKSGIVING

CHOIR—"God Is the Refuge of His Saints."
READER—Ex. 15: 1, 2, 20, 21.
      Ex. 16: 1-3 (explanatory).

SCENE 9

GATHERING MANNA

CHOIR—"Guide Me, O Thou Great Jehovah."
READER—Ex. 16: 11-18.
      Ex. 19: 1-5; 20: 23, 24 (explanatory).

SCENE 10

THE GOLDEN CALF

CHOIR—"My Soul, Be on Thy Guard."
READER—Ex. 32: 1-6.
      Ex. 32: 7, 8 (explanatory).

SCENE 11

Moses Is Angered

CHOIR—"God the All-merciful."
READER—Ex. 32: 15, 19-21.
Ex. 32: 30-35; 33: 1-3; 34: 1, 2; Num. 13: 1-3; 17-20 (explanatory).

SCENE 12

Return of the Spies

CHOIR—"God of Our Fathers, Whose Almighty Hand."
READER—Num. 13: 26-33.

SCENE 13

The Good Report of Caleb and Joshua

CHOIR—"All People that on Earth Do Dwell."
READER—Num. 14: 1-10.
Num. 14: 11, 12, 21-23, 30; Deut. 5: 1-5 (explanatory).

SCENE 14

The Commandments Renewed

CHOIR—"Go to the Deeps of God's Promises."
READER—Deut. 5: 6-21.
Deut. 10: 1-5; 31: 1-3 (explanatory).

SCENE 15

Moses Ordains Joshua

CHOIR—"We Bless Thee for Thy Peace, O God."
READER—Deut. 31: 7, 8.
Deut. 32: 48-52 (explanatory).

SCENE 16

Moses Views the Promised Land

Choir—"A Mighty Fortress Is Our God."
Reader—Deut. 34: 1-12.

TABLEAUX

SCENE 1

The Brick Yards in Egypt: Outdoor Scene. Tall palms at rear right and left. Piles of bricks and straw in center. Several Hebrew Slaves at work. Taskmaster stands with folded arms.

SCENE 2

By the River Side: Row of low palms and ferns or other greenery along back of stage to represent thicket along bank of river. Ziba is in front center, handing the little ark to Jochebed. Little Miriam stands near her mother, and Taptha and Basham stand at right.

SCENE 3

The Brick Yards of Egypt: Same as Scene 1. Taskmaster is beating one of the Slaves. Moses stands watching.

SCENE 4

Jethro's Camp in Midian: Outdoor scene. If possible, have a brown or striped tent at one side of stage, or hang a piece of striped awning to represent the front of a tent, with a roof effect in front. Jethro sits under the awning roof. Moses stands in front of him at a distance. The Daughters are in a group at opposite side, watching.

SCENE 5

On Mount Horeb: Trees and shrubs at right and left. One large bush in center, with red light arranged inside it. ANGEL stands behind it, and MOSES at one side. ANGEL has a staff.

SCENE 6

In Pharaoh's Courtroom: Arrange as elaborately as possible, with PHARAOH seated on elevation at one side. An ATTENDANT stands on each side, holding large fan. Rich canopy above. MOSES and AARON stand down in front, the former with hands extended pleadingly.

SCENE 7

In Pharaoh's Courtroom: Same setting as before. PHARAOH's dead SON lies on steps of throne at his feet. MOSES and AARON stand before him. OFFICERS OF THE COURT stand at opposite side.

SCENE 8

The Wilderness of Shur: Outdoor scene. DANCING MAIDENS in center, with musical instruments uplifted, as if playing upon them. Group of ISRAELITES surround them. MOSES and AARON stand at opposite sides, front, hands clasped, as if in prayer.

SCENE 9

The Wilderness of Sin: Outdoor scene, as before. Group of ISRAELITES stooping over, as if gathering manna. Several are standing, holding platters heaped high with the manna.

SCENE 10

The Plain Near Mount Sinai: The golden calf is on high altar, surrounded by dancing ISRAELITES. They have garlands of flowers, some of which are draped upon the calf and altar. The calf may be made by gilding a child's hobby-horse, or making a larger one from clay, which is dried and then gilded. AARON stands watching them.

SCENE 11

The Plain Near Mount Sinai: Same setting as above. The calf has been knocked from the altar and broken (simply remove it from the scene so it may be used again, and scatter bits of wood on the platform). MOSES stands upon elevation at left, with arms uplifted, as though he had just thrown the tablets. Some of the ISRAELITES are grouped at rear and sides of stage, as though having retreated from his anger, and with arms extended as if to protect themselves from his wrath. Others are pleading before him upon their knees. AARON stands before him with clasped hands.

SCENE 12

The Camp of the Israelites: Outdoor scene, with group of ISRAELITES at one side. The SPIES stand in a group at opposite side. Two of them carry a large bunch of grapes suspended from a pole across their shoulders. The grapes may be secured from a large department or millinery store and several bunches arranged together. MOSES at rear.

SCENE 13

The Camp of the Israelites: Same setting as above. CALEB and JOSHUA stand in center, with arms extended, as though telling about the country.

SCENE 14

The Camp of the Israelites: ISRAELITES are seated. MOSES stands on an elevation, with the tablets of stone (cardboard) in his arms, pointing with one hand to the Commandments written thereon.

SCENE 15

The Camp of the Israelites: Group of ISRAELITES at right. MOSES stands at left, with his right hand upon the head of JOSHUA, who kneels before him.

SCENE 16

On Mount Nebo: MOSES stands alone on an elevation, shielding his eyes as if looking over the land below him.

The Land of All Nations

A PAGEANT OF AMERICA AND THE NEW AMERICANS

CHARACTERS

SPIRIT OF AMERICA (Reader).
SPIRIT OF BROTHERHOOD (Reader).
REPRESENTATIVES OF THE NATIONS.

COSTUMES

SPIRIT OF AMERICA.

White robe with drapery of patriotic colors and a low crown of gold paper.

SPIRIT OF BROTHERHOOD.

Robe of bright color, with wreath of flowers around head.

REPRESENTATIVES OF NATIONS.

See section of "National Costumes." There should be at least two —a man and woman—from each nation, but use as many as possible.

ARRANGEMENT

Special scenery is not needed, but a background of American flags will be effective. Folding screens may be placed on each side, forming entrances. One curtain in front is necessary.

The NATIONAL REPRESENTATIVES take their positions while choir sings, standing at salute, right and left, before a central flag on the rear wall, with one side of body toward audience. When their tableau is completed they retire, each group alternately, to rear right and left, being a part of the next tableau. A spotlight may be used on each national group, while they stand at salute, if desired.

The two READERS have manuscript in book or scroll form.

PAGEANT

TRUMPET SOLO [*behind scenes*]—"America," followed by:

SONG BY AUDIENCE AND CHOIR [*with organ and trumpet*]—"America."

AMERICA [*standing at right of platform*]—We have been singing one of our popular national anthems with an apparent evidence of fervor and enthusiasm; but while our hearts may be stirred by the lovely melody, I am wondering if we really appreciate the meaning of the words, "Sweet land of liberty; land of the noble free." Those who were born in this country and have always enjoyed the blessing of freedom perhaps do not appreciate this privilege as do those who came here seeking freedom from lands where they were oppressed. Zangwill's term, "the melting pot," applies well to America. Within our broad borders all the races of the world come together and are fused into a civilization the like of which the world has never before seen. Our population is becoming marked by the good qualities of all human races, and it also has a chance to be marred by their bad qualities. Sometimes we speak of them as "our new Americans," but all of us, except the Indians, are "new Americans." Some arrived from England, from Holland, from Sweden, from Italy, a few scores of years before the others, but the so-called "new Americans" are only a little newer than all other Americans, except the Indians. The new Americans are absolutely essential to the prosperity of this country. For decades they have been doing the hard work of the nation—building the railroads, digging the sewers, mining the coal. They have freed millions of us for the brain work of the country by doing for us the work of the brawn. But the new Americans also have brain work to contribute. They come from the talented races of the world, races that have given the world its greatest artists, musicians, sculptors, poets, architects. They have much to contribute to the higher life of our country. We have much to learn from them, and they from us. Together we shall go on to make America truly great. Tonight we are to visualize some of these people who have come to "the land of all nations," and thereby strive to get a higher appreciation of their merits. In some cases we will hear their national sacred hymns which we often use in our various churches. But first let us bow our heads while the choir sings our prayer.

CHOIR—"Lord, While for All Mankind We Pray."

SCENE 1—INDIANS

BROTHERHOOD—The Spirit of America has tersely remarked that all of us, except the Indians, are "new Americans." After centuries of oppression at the hands of the white man the Indian is at last coming into his own, is receiving his natural wealth in land, and is entering on terms of full equality with the great body of American citizens. This brave and splendid race has already given a good account of itself, and nowhere better than in our legislative halls. The Indian excels in oratory. He becomes a good farmer. He is capable of the conduct of large affairs. He belongs to an ancient race, but it is not at all decadent. All over the West there are encouraging Protestant missions among the Indians which produce Christians of the very noblest type.

CHOIR—"God Bless Our Native Land."

SCENE 2—POLES

BROTHERHOOD—Perhaps one of the largest groups of immigrants in our country are from Poland, the census reporting their number as nearly three millions. For the most part they are honest and hard-working people, a very important factor in our industrial life. They are nominally Roman Catholic, but about one-third of them have no affiliation with that church, and Protestant work among them would be very successful. Many thousands of these Poles are found in our factories and mines, but on the whole they are an agricultural people, and all over the nation they own their farms, the women and children aiding the men with their labor. They are very independent and do not mix socially with their neighbors or take any decided part in politics.

CHOIR—"O for a Thousand Tongues to Sing."

SCENE 3—AUSTRIANS AND HUNGARIANS

BROTHERHOOD—For a number of years before the World War, Austria-Hungary furnished two-fifths of all our immigrants, and the immigration from these lands (now separated) is still very heavy. About two millions of our citizens come from this part of Europe. From this general region come the Slovaks, Croatians, Ruthenians, Magyars, Moravians and numerous others—Greek Catholics, Roman Catholics and Protestants. They are, many of them, from lands that are proud of a great history, lands that have accomplished much in literature and art, that possess magnificent buildings and great universities. Many of them may be poor and ignorant, but they are of a noble ancestry, and our country will make a woeful mistake if it does not cherish them and develop their fine possibilities.

CHOIR—"Glorious Things of Thee Are Spoken."

SCENE 4—BOHEMIANS

BROTHERHOOD—Bohemia, the land of Huss, will always be a country of profound interest to the Protestant world.

That land first contributed to America those noble people, the Moravians. The country was once very powerful, and at one time was strongly Protestant. It was forced into the Roman Catholic faith at the point of the sword, but its loyalty to that church is lukewarm, and the Bohemians of America are greatly inclined toward infidelity, although they are very open to Protestant work. Bohemian immigrants are to a large extent skilled workmen, and hundreds take readily to farming, ranking high as agriculturists. They also are artistic and musical, and many are successful in business.

CHOIR—"Faith of Our Fathers."

SCENE 5—ITALIANS

BROTHERHOOD—There are more than a million Italians with us, most of them having come from southern Italy. They are a very friendly race, of magnificent ancestry and history. Once the rulers of the world, they have not forgotten how to govern, and they are a power in the politics of many of our large cities. They are good farmers, and in some regions monopolize the fruit industry. They are remarkably good workers and are very thrifty. Great lovers of music and of art, they have made notable contributions to American life. They are devoted to their families, are lovers of liberty, and America has no more loyal citizens than they. Nominally Roman Catholic, they are open to Protestant missions.

CHOIR—"Christ for the World We Sing."

SCENE 6—ARMENIANS

BROTHERHOOD—The Armenians, originating in Asiatic Turkey and driven thence by cruel persecutions and horrible massacres, have come to this country from many other lands, there being more than eighty thousand of them with us.

They are a splendid race of mountain people, keen of intellect, ready of resource, very industrious, and perhaps the brightest traders in the world. They value education highly, and take high rank in the professions and arts. They usually succeed better than any other race of immigrants in accumulating property. While Armenians as a race belong to the Greek Catholic Church, many of them were won by our missionaries before fleeing to America from Turkey, and, upon arriving here, joined Protestant churches.

CHOIR—"From Every Stormy Wind."

SCENE 7—GREEKS

BROTHERHOOD—The estimated number of Greeks in this country is from three hundred thousand to half a million, and they are widely distributed throughout the states. About twenty-five thousand of them live in New York City. They are industrious and prosperous, being very keen in business. Some of them have become millionaires. They are especially successful as fruit dealers, keepers of restaurants, grocers, bankers and managers of shoe-shine establishments. They are temperate and eager to get an education. The women usually help their husbands in their work. They are orderly and loyal to the Government. Their religion is the Greek Catholic, but they are open to Protestant missions.

CHOIR—"Crown Him with Many Crowns."

SCENE 8—RUSSIANS

BROTHERHOOD—From a land of century-long oppression the Russians come to labor in our mines, factories and workshops. They are a patient people, ready to work hard and long for low wages. They are very religious, but worship God through sacred pictures, or *icons*. They are musical and artistic, and their children often take high rank in our public schools. They are charitable and generous, in spite of their poverty.

CHOIR—"God, the All-merciful."

SCENE 9—FRENCH, SWISS, PORTUGUESE AND SPANISH

BROTHERHOOD—Latin Europe has sent us more than a hundred thousand immigrants from both France and Switzerland, with some sixty thousand Portuguese and a small number of Spanish, but these countries have contributed less to our country's population than we could wish. They are home-loving people and do not care to leave their own delightful lands.

CHOIR—"How Firm a Foundation."

SCENE 10—IRISH

BROTHERHOOD—Ireland, especially during its years of famine, sent us many hundreds of thousands of its most enterprising citizens. For a time they did the drudgery of our country. Now they run many of our large cities through the exercise of their talents for politics, and have become a strong factor in the commercial and literary life of the United States. Most of them are devout Catholics, although those from the north of Ireland and from Canada being equally strong Protestants.

CHOIR—"O God, Our Help in Ages Past."

SCENE 11—BRITISH

BROTHERHOOD—Great Britain has sent hundreds of thousands of people to our country and they are scattered in every state. These English, Scotch and Welsh people have brought to us the pioneer principles on which our many denominations are founded, and have brought many ministers to our modern churches. These people are of a quiet disposition and are loyal to our country in all of its demands. They have contributed much in music and literature.

CHOIR—"God Is the Refuge of His Saints."

SCENE 12—GERMANS AND HOLLANDERS

BROTHERHOOD—Very early in the history of our country the Germans began immigrating to us and have been among the most loyal and trustworthy citizens. Largely of the Lutheran faith, although mingled with many of the Evangelical, Methodist and Reformed, they have established hundreds of churches throughout our land. Their appreciation of music and art is very high and they contribute a delightful element to American civilization. The Hollanders have not come to us in large numbers, and are a lovable people, who have established their own churches and are very devout. They are found largely in the rural districts, being chiefly engaged in agriculture and dairying.

CHOIR—"A Mighty Fortress Is Our God."

SCENE 13—SCANDINAVIANS AND DANES

BROTHERHOOD—There are thousands of people from Norway, Sweden and Denmark in our country, and they are among our most loyal and industrious citizens. They have given us the best of their brains and hearts and hands. They have helped fight our battles—military and political. They have entered into our commercial life, but most of them are engaged in agriculture and dairying, and are scattered over the central and north-central states. Nearly all of them are Protestants, and their faith is as strong as their works are many and admirable.

CHOIR—"O Lord of Heaven and Earth and Sea."

SCENE 14—JEWS

BROTHERHOOD—Our country has become the true home of the Jew. This great race, which gave to the world the Bible and Christianity, began to come here long before the Revolution, and they have proved themselves loyal in all our wars. They have furnished America with some conspicuously able and useful Congressmen, Senators, judges and members of the Cabinet. The power of the Jew in finance is well known, though Jews are not so rich as is popularly supposed. The Jews are law-abiding, charitable and take good care of their own people. They are a brilliant race, and they furnish many of America's leading poets, novelists, dramatists, painters, musicians, editors, inventors, doctors, lawyers and scientists. They have found the moving picture a most congenial field for their genius, and have almost monopolized it. Protestant work among them bears rich fruit when it is tried, which is all too seldom.

CHOIR—"O God, Our Help in Ages Past."

SCENE 15—MEXICANS AND CUBANS

BROTHERHOOD—It is believed that there are more than a million Mexicans in our country, besides those born here of Mexican parents. Most of them are in the Southwestern states. Our missionaries have to contend with their ignorance and superstition and the influence of their priests. They are enslaved by ancient customs, many of them evil, and there is much immorality among them. Protestant missions have produced surprising results. In addition to these Latin Americans, there are thousands of Cubans in Florida, and the entire island of Porto Rico, with its population of a million, is under our flag. Since it was taken over by our country a veritable transformation for the better has been wrought.

CHOIR—"Holy Ghost with Light Divine."

SCENE 16—NEGROES

BROTHERHOOD—One-ninth of our population belongs to the black race, and the Negro is therefore a tremendous factor in American life. He also is fast becoming a powerful factor in our commercial life. He is making great progress in education and already owns a large number of farms. He is constantly building better homes, learning all trades and educating himself in all professions. In music and poetry he has made distinct and original contributions to American life. He has a kindly, gentle, winsome spirit, and his deep religious feeling is unexcelled by any race within our borders.

CHOIR—"Steal Away to Jesus" [*or other spiritual*].

SCENE 17—ASIATIC IMMIGRANTS

BROTHERHOOD—Before the number of immigrants from Asia was sharply cut off, we took into our country thousands of Chinese, Japanese, Turks and a few Hindus. They have settled mostly along the Pacific Coast, which is nearest their native shores, although many have migrated eastward into our larger cities. They have engaged in laundry work, domestic work and hotel work, but many also have laid our railroads and have tilled many farms. Our mission work among them is limited, but bears splendid fruit wherever promoted.

CHOIR—"In Christ There Is No East or West."

AMERICA—

> I love my country's pine-clad hills,
> Her thousand limpid gushing rills,
>   Her sunshine and her storms;
> Her rough and rugged rocks that rear
> Their hoary heads high in the air,
>   In proud majestic forms.

78

I love her rivers, deep and wide,
Those mighty streams that seaward glide,
  To seek the ocean's breast;
Her smiling fields, her pleasant vales,
Her shady dells, her flow'ry dales,
  The haunts of peaceful rest.

I love her forests, dark and lone,
For there the wild bird's merry tone
  Is heard from morn till night;
And there are lovelier flowers, I ween,
That ne'er in Eastern lands were seen,
  In varied colors bright.

Her forests and her valleys fair,
Her flowers that scent the morning air,
  Have all their charms for me;
But more I love my country's name,
Those words that echo deathless fame—
  The Land of Liberty!   —*Author Unknown.*

CHOIR—"Lord, While for All Mankind We Pray."

SCENE 18—THE LAND OF ALL NATIONS

[*All characters grouped on platform, in tiers, if possible, while all join in closing songs, waving flags.*]

CHOIR AND ALL CHARACTERS—"Columbia, Gem of the Ocean" [*wave American flags; one verse only*]; "We've a Story to Tell to the Nations" [*wave foreign flags*].

The Messengers

Or

VISIONS OF THE PROPHETS

CHARACTERS

FIRST READER.	JONAH.
SECOND READER.	MICAH.
ISAIAH.	NAHUM.
JEREMIAH.	HABAKKUK.
EZEKIEL.	ZEPHANIAH.
DANIEL.	HAGGAI.
HOSEA.	ZECHARIAH.
JOEL.	MALACHI.
AMOS.	MEN AND WOMEN.
OBADIAH.	OFFICIALS.
ANGEL.	

COSTUMES

The costumes are the typical Hebrew garments of Bible days, and may be prepared from bathrobes, dressing gowns, shawls, scarfs, window draperies, nightgowns, sheets, etc. Modern women's outing flannel nightgowns make excellent tunics for Hebrew men, and sheets also can be used, with scarfs draped over left shoulder and pinned under right arm. All of the men should wear beards, which can be made from crepe hair applied with theatrical art gum. Headdresses are made from 24-inch squares of cloth, tied in hood effect with a cord. Legs should be bare and bedroom slippers worn. AMOS is a shepherd and MICAH a peasant. WOMEN wear flowing robes of various colors, with soft veils around head and hanging down back.

6   81

ARRANGEMENT

Special scenery is not needed, but a few tall palms to use in the background of some of the scenes will add variety. If possible, have a tarlatan curtain on front of stage to give the scenes a deep effect. The characters stand motionless while story is read. The NARRATOR has a scroll on which manuscript is pasted. Scenes are changed while songs are being sung.

PAGEANT

FIRST READER—In making a study of the Old Testament, we find that the thirty-nine books are divided into three groups—historical, poetical and prophetical. Sixteen prophets are responsible for the latter group. These prophets belong to the dark days of Israel's history, the period of the nation's decay, even as the poetical books belong to the golden age. Eleven of these prophets lived in the era of the nation's destruction, and included Jonah, Joel, Amos, Hosea, Isaiah, Micah, Jeremiah, Nahum, Habakkuk, Zephaniah and Obadiah. The two who lived during the Babylonian captivity were Ezekiel and Daniel, while the three who prophesied during the era of restoration were Haggai, Zechariah and Malachi. The whole period covered about four hundred years, 800-400 B. C.

SECOND READER—Prophets seem to have first appeared in the days of Samuel, in connection with the change in the government, the organization of the kingdom and the shake-up in the priesthood. They did not inherit office as the priests did, but each one was called of God for some special work. They were often political advisers, as well as preachers of righteousness and predictors of events. Samuel organized the kingdom; Nathan helped build it up; Ahijah aided in dividing it; Elijah and Elisha led in the grand fight against Baal worship, the most horrible form of idolatry into which the nation ever fell.

FIRST READER—The mission and message of the later prophets were fivefold: (1) To save the nation from its idolatry and wickedness. Then, failing to do this, to announce that (2) the nation, because of its idolatry, will be destroyed; (3) but a remnant will be saved; (4) out of which will come an influence that will bring all nations to Jehovah; (5) that influence will be a great Man in the family of David.

It is the purpose of the service this evening to study the lessons of the sixteen prophets and to visualize their messages. However, we will make this study in the chronological order of the dates they lived, rather than the order in which they are arranged in the Old Testament.

SCENE 1

[JONAH *preaching in Nineveh; group kneeling.*]

SECOND READER—Jonah succeeded Elisha as God's messenger to the ten tribes. At that time the Jews were divided in their attitude toward other nations. Some believed that they were a chosen people, that their religion was for themselves alone, and that they should keep themselves apart from heathen nations. They felt that in due time God would crush the Gentiles and make the Jews the masters of the world. Others believed that, since the Jews had the true religion, it was their duty to share it with the heathen. Jonah belonged to the selfish group, and he rebelled when he heard the command of God, "Arise, go to Nineveh, that great city, and cry against it; for their wickedness is come up before me." Instead of obeying, he went to the seaport city, Joppa, and took passage in a ship going to Tarshish, which probably was in Spain, seeking thus to escape from his obligation. But, being overtaken by a storm on the Mediterranean, he was cast into the sea, swallowed by a great fish, and from inside the fish, earnestly praying to God for three days, he was delivered. At the renewed command of God he went to Nineveh and began to preach a very simple sermon: "Yet forty days, and Nineveh shall be overthrown." The people believed his words, proclaimed a fast, and put on sackcloth in humility. Even the king arose from his throne, laid his robe from him, covered himself with sackcloth and sat in ashes. "And God saw their works, that they turned from their evil way; and God repented of the evil which he said he would do unto them; and he did it not." Jonah, fearing to be regarded as a false prophet, repined at the mercy of God and wished for death. Leaving the city, he was sheltered by a gourd, which is eaten by a worm and shortly withered; and Jonah, manifesting great impatience and rebellion, is shown through his concern about the gourd, the propriety of God's mercy to Nineveh. Undoubtedly the great purpose of the Book of Jonah was to teach Israel that no man can find a hideaway from conscience nor from God, and that no nation, knowing God, dare keep Him to themselves.

SONG—"God Moves in a Mysterious Way."

SCENE 2

[JOEL *addressing a group of people.*]

FIRST READER—Joel was a prophet in Jerusalem, probably during the reign of Joash. A terrible plague of locusts, followed by a prolonged and severe drought, was devastating the land. The prophet takes this as the sign of a more terrible judgment to come upon the nations, to be followed or accompanied by the outpouring of God's Spirit upon the nations, an era in which the nations shall be given a chance to turn to Jehovah; those who repent will be saved, while those who refuse will bring judgment upon themselves. Thus spake the prophet: "The Lord also shall roar out of Zion, and utter his voice from Jerusalem; and the heavens and the earth shall shake: but the Lord will be the hope of his people, and the strength of the children of Israel."

SONG—"O God, Our Help in Ages Past."

SCENE 3

[AMOS *addressing a group of people.*]

SECOND READER—Some years later there came an era of prosperity in Israel, resulting in dissensions between the powerful and the weak, the rich and the poor. Jeroboam II was king, and he extended his kingdom by military conquests. But there was much dishonesty, and while the rich reveled in luxury many were starving. Then out of the desert of Tekoa came the bearded, browned Amos, as God's thunderer over Israel, for by profession he was a herdsman and a dresser of sycomore trees. He rebuked, among other things, the corruption of the people's manners, which kept pace with their prosperity; he charged the great men with partiality as judges, and violence toward the poor; and foretold, as a punishment from God, the captivity of the ten tribes in a foreign country, a prediction accomplished about sixty years later. "Thus saith the Lord unto the house of Israel, Seek ye me, and ye shall live. Seek him that maketh the seven stars and Orion; and turneth the shadow of death into morning, and maketh the day dark with night; that calleth for the waters of the sea, and poureth them upon the face of the earth: the Lord is his name."

SONG—"There's a Wideness in God's Mercy."

SCENE 4

[HOSEA *speaking to a group of people.*]

FIRST READER—Hosea was a prophet who warned Israel, foretold her overthrow and pointed to the latter days. The spirit of idolatry had continued for more than 150 years and was beginning to yield anarchy and decay. God had sent Elijah and Elisha and Jonah, but in vain. Kings and princes were murderers and profligates. The idolatrous priests had spread their shameful festivals and deceitful oracles all over the land. God and His Word were forgotten. These conditions the prophet earnestly condemns, using facts of his own sad domestic history to reprove their idolatry. He compares this to the relationship between Jehovah and His people. Among the more remarkable of his predictions are those in which he foretells the downfall of Samaria, with the captivities and sufferings of Israel; the punishment of Judah and her cities; the eventual conversion of Israel and her union with Judah; and the final ransom of God's people from death. Thus he speaks unto the people: "O Israel, return unto the Lord thy God; for thou hast fallen by thine iniquity. Who is wise shall understand these things; prudent, and he shall know them; for the ways of the Lord are right, and the just shall walk in them: but the transgressors shall fall therein."

SONG—"All People that on Earth Do Dwell."

SCENE 5

[ISAIAH *speaking to a group of people.*]

SECOND READER—Isaiah, greatest of the prophets, was active in the reigns of Uzziah, Jotham, Ahaz and Hezekiah. As a young man he had a vision and heard a call; he warned Judah of the judgment to come; he fought bitterly the kings who left Jehovah to put their trust in foreign alliances, and he strove to call the people from blasphemous sacrifices to genuine justice and humanity. The sign of "Immanuel" is given to reassure the king and people. Isaiah is quoted in the New Testament more than any other prophet. What a mind he had! In some of his rhapsodies he reaches heights of sublimity unequaled by Shakespeare, Milton or Homer.

"Come now and let us reason together, saith the Lord: though your sins be as scarlet, they shall be white as snow: though they be red like crimson, they shall be as wool.

"Also I heard the voice of the Lord saying, Whom shall I send and who will go for us? Then said I, Here am I; send me.

"Ye are my witnesses, saith the Lord, and my servants whom I have chosen: that ye may know and believe me, and understand that I am he: before me there was no God formed, neither shall there be any after me.

"Seek ye the Lord while he may be found; call ye upon him while he is near: Let the wicked forsake his way, and the unrighteous man his thoughts: and let him return unto the Lord, and he will have mercy upon him; and to our God, for he will abundantly pardon.

"For my thoughts are not your thoughts, neither are my ways your ways, saith the Lord. For as the heavens are higher than the earth, so are my ways higher than your ways, and my thoughts than your thoughts."

SONG—"God of Our Fathers, Known of Old."

SCENE 6

[MICAH *speaking to a group of people.*]

FIRST READER—Micah was a contemporary of Isaiah, but their natures were far different—Isaiah was a prince, cultured and refined; Micah was a peasant, a man of the people and champion of the poor. He stepped forth alone from the ranks of the oppressed to denounce the oppressor. He mourned the lack of justice for the poor, rebuked and threatened the princes, false prophets and people for their sins. National calamity was sure to come, Micah declared.

"Therefore shall Zion be plowed as a field, Jerusalem shall become heaps." But after that should come the Messiah. Twice he reached great heights. Once he talked of the nations beating their swords into plowshares and their spears into pruning hooks. Again he asked, "What doth the Lord require of thee but to do justly, and to love mercy, and to walk humbly with thy God?" Micah is the only one of the prophets that names Bethlehem as the birthplace of the Messiah. It is his contribution to the ever increasing fund of prophetic explanations as to how Israel is going to accomplish its Messianic mission.

SONG—"O Lord of Heaven and Earth and Sea."

SCENE 7

[JEREMIAH *preaching to a group of people.*]

SECOND READER—During the reign of the young king, Josiah, the people of Judah were thrown into terror by the appearance of a fierce horde of Scythians that swept down from the north, carrying destruction wherever they went. Then came Jeremiah from a village near Jerusalem, declaring that God was using the Scythians to punish the land for the wickedness of the people, for God said: "I will utter my judgments against them, touching all their wickedness, in that they have forsaken me, and have burned incense unto other gods, and worshipped the works of their own hands." But the Scythians went down the coast to the border of Egypt, and returned northward the same route, without bothering Judah.

Jeremiah got his message to the people by speaking in the temple to the throngs that came to the feasts, sometimes doing symbolic things to attract attention, like wearing a certain kind of girdle, putting a yoke on his neck, or breaking a bottle. He buried his clothes and dug them up. He said to Judah, "Your faith is like that; once it was white and clean, but now, buried, mouldy. You drone vain words about the temple, but your temple is a fetish, your faith a magical farce. Return, ye backsliding children; you may gain Jehovah's favor by a change of life, by obeying his law."

All through the years Jeremiah preached, prophesied and warned of the coming exile, pleading for a heart set right with God before the end. He saw his people scattered, and uttered his lamentations over the fall of the city; then he died. But he predicted a new covenant, a day when God's law would be written on Jewish hearts instead of Jewish books. "In that day, saith the Lord, they shall all know me, from the least of them unto the greatest of them; for I will forgive their iniquity and I will remember their sin no more."

Song—" 'Tis by the Faith of Joys to Come."

SCENE 8

[Nahum *is addressing a group of people.*]

First Reader—Nahum was a prophet in Judah. After the fall of Samaria he foretells the destruction of Nineveh, which at that time was the capital of the great and flourishing Assyrian Empire, being center of the principal commerce of the world. But it plundered the neighboring nations and is compared by the prophet to a family of lions. It was strongly fortified. Its colossal walls are reported as being one hundred feet high, and wide enough at the top for three chariots to be driven abreast on them, with fifteen hundred towers bidding defiance to all enemies. Yet, in accordance with the prophecy of Nahum, it was so totally destroyed by the Medes and Babylonians that in the second century after Christ not a vestige remained of it, and its very site was long a matter of uncertainty. Thus spake Nahum unto them:

"The Lord is slow to anger, and great in power; the Lord hath his way in the whirlwind and in the storm, and the clouds are the dust of his feet. The Lord is good, a stronghold in the day of trouble; and he knoweth them that trust him."

SONG—"God, the All-merciful."

SCENE 9

[HABAKKUK *is speaking to an assembly of people.*]

SECOND READER—Habakkuk was contemporary with Jeremiah and prophesied on the Chaldean invasion and the return of the Jews to Jerusalem. Habakkuk saw the prophecy of Nahum fulfilled, and saw the Chaldean become a more cruel tyrant over Judah than the Assyrian. He wondered how God could allow such a condition. In a vision God answers that Babylon and her gods would yet be destroyed, and Jehovah should eventually prevail over the earth. "For, said he, the earth shall be filled with the knowledge of the glory of the Lord, as the waters cover the sea." One theme of his message is that "the just shall live by faith." He pronounces five "woes" upon the Chaldeans: for insatiate ambition, for unscrupulous greed, for injustice and cruelty, for drunken debauchery and for gross idolatry. He concludes with a sublime song, both of praise and of prayer, designed to afford consolation to the pious Jews under their approaching calamities.

SONG—"God Is the Refuge of His Saints."

SCENE 10

[ZEPHANIAH *preaching to a group of people.*]

FIRST READER—Following the prophecies of Isaiah, Micah and Nahum, there was an interval of fifty years, during which there was no prophet whose writings have reached us. The wicked reign of Manasseh occupied nearly all of this period. With King Josiah, however, the prophetic spirit revived and Zephaniah is the earliest prophet of that age. He probably assisted Josiah in destroying the altars of Baal and restoring the worship of Jehovah. He prophesied against various nations and predicted the restoration. "I will utterly consume all things from off the land, saith the Lord, and them that are turned back from the Lord; and those that have not sought the Lord. Seek ye the Lord, all ye meek of the earth, which have wrought his judgment; seek righteousness, seek meekness: it may be ye shall be hid in the day of the Lord's anger."

SONG—"God Will Take Care of You."

SCENE 11

[OBADIAH *standing alone, with upraised fist.*]

SECOND READER—When the Babylonians destroyed Jerusalem they were assisted by the Edomites, who were descendants of Esau, and who dwelt in the rocky, almost impregnable country south of the Dead Sea. Like their father Esau, they were profane, without religion. They always were bitter enemies of the Jews, continuing the enmity between Esau and Jacob, and always ready to help an attacking army. While the Babylonians sacked Jerusalem, the Edomites stood on the surrounding hills and encouraged its destruction. So Obadiah shook his fist toward the horizon, toward Edom, and sang a hymn of hate to the Edomites. He rebukes their heartless treatment of the Jews, for all of which an early day of retribution was to come. "As thou hast done, it shall be done unto thee," he declared. Obadiah wept not tears of despair; he was mad, and his uncontrolled anger made him the least of the minor prophets. But the closing line of his message reveals a finer man. "The kingdom shall be the Lord's," he says. That sounds much like "Thy kingdom come." Jehovah's religion will yet be triumphant.

SONG—"Guide Me, O Thou Great Jehovah."

SCENE 12

[EZEKIEL *preaching to a group of people.*]

FIRST READER—Ezekiel was a priest as well as a prophet. He was one of the great company of captives carried to Babylon with the young king, Jehoiachin, by Nebuchadnezzar. These captives were distributed into settlements throughout Babylonia, forming small communities, with freedom to worship. The company to which Ezekiel belonged seems to have consisted of well-to-do people, who resisted the words of their priest-prophet, clinging to the hope of a speedy return to the land of their fathers. It was Ezekiel's task to disenchant them and to warn them of the destruction of Jerusalem. "As I live, saith the Lord God, I have no pleasure in the death of the wicked: but that the wicked turn from his way and live: Turn ye, turn ye from your evil ways; for why will ye die, O house of Israel? The soul that sinneth, it shall die. But if the wicked will turn from all his sins, and keep all my statutes, and do that which is lawful and right, he shall surely live and not die." Ezekiel closes his message by revealing his vision of the waters flowing from Jerusalem and blessing the nations.

SONG—"O for a Faith that Will Not Shrink."

SCENE 13

[DANIEL *at prayer upon his knees, with face uplifted; several* OFFICIALS *standing near by.*]

SECOND READER—Daniel was the daring prophet. He was carried captive to Babylon as a youth, and there he was placed in the court of King Nebuchadnezzar, where he became acquainted with the science of the Chaldeans, attaining a wisdom superior to their own. By Nebuchadnezzar he was raised to high rank and great power. He prophesied during the whole of the captivity. A most remarkable man was Daniel to have been so absolutely true to his own religious convictions and yet loyal to his idolatrous king, so he could be trusted with affairs of state of heathen world empires.

The first event which gained Daniel influence in the court was his disclosure and explanation of the king's dream, and several years later a second dream, which was interpreted as foreshadowing his madness. Then came Belshazzar's feast, with the handwriting on the wall. Jealous because of Daniel's popularity and advancement, certain officials conspired with the new king, Darius, to issue a decree which would cast into a den of lions any one who would ask a petition of any god or man for thirty days. "Wherefore king Darius signed the decree. Now when Daniel knew that the writing was signed, he went into his house, and his windows being opened toward Jerusalem, he kneeled three times a day and prayed, and gave thanks before his God, as he did aforetime. Then these men came and found Daniel praying and making supplication before his God." The irrevocable decree must be kept, but God sent His angels to shut the lions' mouths, and Daniel was restored, while his accusers were cast unto the lions.

"Then king Darius wrote unto all the people, nations and languages that dwell in all the earth, Peace be multiplied unto you. I make a decree: That in every dominion of my kingdom men shall tremble and fear before the God of

Daniel; for he is the living God, and stedfast for ever, and his kingdom that which shall not be destroyed, and his dominion shall be even unto the end."

Attention should also be given to a promise made by God's messenger to Daniel: "They that be wise shall shine as the brightness of the firmament, and they that turn many to righteousness, as the stars for ever and ever."

SONG—"God of Our Fathers, Whose Almighty Hand."

SCENE 14

[HAGGAI *preaching to a group of people.*]

FIRST READER—The permission of Cyrus to rebuild the temple in Jerusalem had for several years borne but little fruit. An altar of burnt offering had been erected and the yearly festivals were observed in a limited way. The foundations of the temple had been laid, but the work had been greatly hindered by the Samaritans and other enemies of the Jews. Then Haggai and Zechariah were raised up by God to stimulate the people to new effort. Haggai's messages were all delivered in about four months. "Thus saith the Lord of hosts; consider your ways. Go up to the mountain and bring wood, and build the house; and I will take pleasure in it, and I will be glorified. Be strong, all ye people of the land, for I am with you. The glory of this latter house shall be greater than of the former; and in this place will I give peace."

SONG—"Awake, My Soul!"

SCENE 15

[*Two men (one in red) are stooping at right, as if measuring the base of a wall. An* ANGEL *is whispering to* ZECHARIAH *at left.*]

94

SECOND READER—Zechariah had the same general purpose as Haggai—to encourage the Jews in rebuilding the temple, which was finally accomplished in about six years. "Turn ye unto me, saith the Lord of hosts, and I will turn unto you." Zechariah went to Jerusalem and discovered the devil and a young man with a measuring stick in hand. He named the devil Satan, made him a cunning tempter. The boy was laying out the lines of a new city wall. An angel whispered to the prophet and said, "Run, speak to this man; tell him to build his temple first, strengthen his soul before his gates; tell him that walls are futile, they shut one in and others out; that God wants expansion, not exclusion." Zechariah is very frequently quoted in the New Testament, and next to Isaiah he has the most frequent foreshadowings of the character and coming of our Lord. "Not by might, nor by power, but by my spirit, saith the Lord of hosts."

SONG—"A Mighty Fortress Is Our God."

SCENE 16

[MALACHI *is preaching to a group.*]

FIRST READER—Malachi is the last of the Old Testament prophets, as Nehemiah is the last of the historians. The second temple was completed and the services of the altar, with its offerings and sacrifices, was established, although perverted and profaned. Both priests and people were delinquent, as Nehemiah found them; and Malachi denounces the very evils which the historian describes. Discouraged by their weakness, they had settled down to wait the coming of the Messiah promised by the prophets. Malachi assures them that the great One will come, but His coming will bring judgment rather than comfort to people like them. But the prophet closes his message with an assurance of approaching salvation, predicts the rising of the Sun of righteousness, and urges until that day the observance of the law. For thus saith the Lord of hosts:

"Behold, I will send my messenger, and he shall prepare the way before me: and the Lord, whom ye seek, shall suddenly come to his temple; but who may abide the day of his coming? and who shall stand when he appeareth? for he is like a refiner's fire, and like fullers' soap: and he shall sit as a refiner and purifier of silver: and he shall purify the sons of Levi, and purge them as gold and silver, that they may offer unto the Lord an offering in righteousness. And I will be a swift witness against the sorcerers, and against the adulterers, and against false swearers, and against those that oppress the hireling in his wages, the widow, and the fatherless, and fear not me. Bring ye all the tithes into the storehouse, that there may be meat in mine house, and prove me now herewith, saith the Lord of hosts, if I will not open the windows of heaven, and pour you out a blessing, that there shall not be room enough to receive it."

SONG—"How Firm a Foundation."

Highway Builders*

A PAGEANT SHOWING THE WORK OF SOME PIONEER HOME MISSIONARIES

CHARACTERS

READERS

SPIRIT OF AMERICA   SPIRIT OF MISSIONS

TABLEAUX

TIMOTHY_____An Early Christian

ELDER BREWSTER_____First Pilgrim Minister

JOHN ELIOT_____First Missionary to the Indians

DAVID BRAINERD_____A Friend of the Red Man

JOHN MASON PECK____A Bringer of Bibles to the West

JASON LEE_____A Colonizer of the Coast

MR. AND MRS. MARCUS WHITMAN____Martyrs of Oregon

SHELDON JACKSON_____The Apostle of Alaska

MRS. A. R. McFARLAND_____A Teacher in Alaska

FRANCIS E. HIGGINS_____The Lumberjacks' Sky Pilot

A GROUP OF EARLY CHRISTIANS.

A GROUP OF PILGRIMS.

A GROUP OF INDIANS.

A GROUP OF POOR FOLKS.

A GROUP OF ALASKANS.

A GROUP OF LUMBERJACKS.

---

* The information regarding most of these leaders is taken from "Missionary Milestones," by Margaret R. Seebach, and is used by permission of the publishers, The Council of Women for Home Missions, New York City.

COSTUMES

TIMOTHY.

See description of Bible costumes in other pageants in this text.

THE MISSIONARIES.

Use old-fashioned costumes copied from pictures.

ELDER BREWSTER AND PILGRIMS.

See section of "National Costumes."

INDIANS AND ALASKANS.

See section of "National Costumes."

LUMBERJACKS.

Coarse clothing of woodsmen.

SPIRIT OF AMERICA.

White dress draped with patriotic colors.

SPIRIT OF MISSIONS.

Modern dress or flowing robe of bright color.

ARRANGEMENT

The narrative is given from books or scrolls read by the SPIRIT OF AMERICA and the SPIRIT OF MISSIONS, standing on opposite sides of stage.

The tableaux may be presented in "still life" or as pantomimes.

The scenes are changed while choir sings.

Other scenes of denominational leaders may be added.

PAGEANT

PRELUDE OF TRUMPETS—"America."

CHOIR [*with trumpets*]—"God of Our Fathers, Whose Almighty Hand."

AMERICA—About nineteen hundred years ago the apostle Paul wrote a challenging letter to leaders of one of the early churches. Let us visualize the group as the letter is read to them by Timothy.

98

SCENE 1

[TIMOTHY *stands before a seated group of* EARLY CHRISTIANS, *with scroll in his hands.*]

MISSIONS [*during tableau*]—"Brethren, I count not myself to have apprehended: but this one thing I do, forgetting those things which are behind, and reaching forth unto those things which are before, I press toward the mark for the prize of the high calling of God in Christ Jesus. Let nothing be done through strife or vainglory, but in lowliness of mind let each esteem others better than themselves. Let this mind be in you, which was also in Christ Jesus, who, being in the form of God, thought it not robbery to be equal with God, but made himself of no reputation and took upon him the form of a servant, and was made in the likeness of men: and being found in fashion as a man, he humbled himself and became obedient unto death, even the death of the cross. Wherefore God also hath highly exalted him, and given him a name which is above every name: that at the name of Jesus every knee should bow, of things in heaven, and things in earth, and things under the earth, and that every tongue should confess that Jesus Christ is Lord, to the glory of God the Father."

CURTAIN

CHOIR—"Ye Servants of God."

AMERICA—It is frequently charged that the Protestant church in America has failed in her mission, in view of the millions yet unchurched. We do not attempt to deny that much more might have been done if all churches had been constantly alive to their duty and opportunity. But those who apply the brand of failure overlook both the immensity of the task and the great work actually accomplished. Missionaries of the cross have not only converted thousands to its standard, but have been the founders of schools, industries, playgrounds, hospitals, social settlements, colleges and universities, in addition to the great chain of churches which they have organized across the continent. In this respect they have been builders of a great highway of service, inspiration and cheer, which has led millions to the very throne of God. Let us therefore visualize the activities of some of these highway builders that we may the more appreciate their sacrifices and the heritage that is ours.

SCENE 2

[*A* GROUP OF PILGRIMS *at prayer. This may be arranged as an outdoor scene, with several evergreen trees sprinkled with cotton snow, or it may be the interior of a church.*]

MISSIONS [*during tableau*]—No historian is needed to relate the coming of the Pilgrims. Celebrated in song, in story, in oratory, in art, the little "Mayflower" has been pictured as the ark of our national deliverance. These English separatists, the ancestors of the modern Congregational church, brought with them their own preachers of the Word. Encouraged by the success of the first Pilgrims, many Puritans followed them to the New World, so that they might find a refuge from persecution and establish their own government. Accordingly, in 1630, under the leadership of John Winthrop, about one thousand persons sailed for Massachusetts, where they planted settlements. Five years later three thousand more came to join them. Elder Brewster was the first minister of these Pilgrims.

CURTAIN

CHOIR—"Faith of Our Fathers."

AMERICA—In those early days the church was the center of community life, and, because they lived thus in small settlements, missionary work among their own group was unnecessary. Therefore their first evangelistic work was amongst those who were the original Americans.

SCENE 3

[JOHN ELIOT *preaching to a* GROUP OF INDIANS, *with outdoor setting.*]

MISSIONS [*during tableau*]—John Eliot, "The Apostle to the Indians," had an excellent education in England, and, after coming to America, he located in Roxbury, Mass., where he preached for nearly sixty years. He came into frequent contact with the Indians, who often came into the villages, and he learned their language from a young Indian, by whose help he also translated the Commandments, the Lord's Prayer and many texts of Scripture. When he began preaching to them many of them soon forsook their heathen worship, prayed with their families and asked for teachers for their children. Eliot taught them to enclose their fields, build houses, spin and make garments, plant gardens and orchards, and organized a total of fourteen Indian settlements. He spent nearly forty years translating and publishing an Indian Bible, the first edition of which comprised fifteen hundred copies.

CURTAIN

CHOIR—"How Firm a Foundation."

AMERICA—The first home missionaries were these pioneer pastors, who, in addition to their regular duties, undertook to give the gospel to the Indians and follow up those settlers who pushed farther inland. The infant church in America felt called of God to see that no settlement, no matter how small or how remote, was destitute of gospel privileges. So the pastors spent many weeks on long journeys into the wilderness.

SCENE 4

[DAVID BRAINERD *standing with a* GROUP OF INDIANS *around their camp fire. The same* INDIANS *of last scene may be used.*]

MISSIONS [*during tableau*]—The story of David Brainerd, young missionary to the Indians, is filled with both pathos and devotion. Expelled from college because he would not apologize for remarks made about the religious faith of some member of the faculty, he was granted a license to preach and became a missionary among the Indians in the region of the Delaware and Susquehanna Rivers. Never of robust health, he was frequently taken ill from exposure. He was often lost in the woods and obliged to spend the night in the open in disagreeable weather. We can hardly realize to-day the desolate and barren regions through which he rode. His inexperience with the language, split into many dialects, and the ignorance of the Indians, were among his difficulties. But the Indians came to trust him and he made many friends with them. Once he came upon a group having a pow-wow, dancing wildly around the medicine man. But David went into the midst of them and finally led them to forsake their heathen worship. In addition to his spiritual work, he had all their worldly affairs on his hands, visiting their wigwams which were filled with smoke and filth. He died in the home of Jonathan Edwards, at the early age of twenty-nine years.

CURTAIN

CHOIR—"Jesus, I My Cross Have Taken."

AMERICA—As the line of occupation was pushed farther and farther inland, the task of evangelism became too great for the individual churches, and home missionary societies began to be formed.

SCENE 5

[JOHN MASON PECK *conducting a Sunday school for* POOR FOLKS.]

MISSIONS [*during tableau*]—John Mason Peck, son of a Connecticut farmer, became a preacher in New York State; was drawn to home mission work by reading David Brainerd's "Memoirs" and by learning of the spiritual needs of the newly acquired Louisiana Purchase; and in 1817 started west with his family in a one-horse wagon. After crossing Ohio, they had to leave the wagon and travel by boat. Reaching St. Louis, they found an unchurched population, an open Sunday and a scarcity of Bibles. Peck first secured a box of Bibles from Connecticut, then rented a room and began preaching and teaching, presently organizing a church, a day school and a Sunday school for Negroes. Later he traveled through Illinois and Missouri, often among people of the poorest "squatter" type. In three years he established over fifty schools. He became an agent for the American Bible Society, and distributed many copies of the Scriptures. He began the publication of a religious newspaper, *The Pioneer*, and helped establish the Baptist Home Missionary Society.

CURTAIN

CHOIR—"Take the Name of Jesus with You."

AMERICA—When the leaders of home mission enterprises met to consider the promotion of the gospel to those settlers who were scattered over Ohio and the regions beyond, little did they realize the magnitude of their undertaking. The population at that time was about five millions, practically all within a hundred miles of the coast, and the western boundary being the Mississippi River. But as new states were added and new trails opened, the highway builders were ready to enter the fields.

SCENE 6

[JASON LEE *preaching to a* GROUP OF INDIANS, *or making furniture while* INDIANS *watch. Outdoor scene.*]

MISSIONS [*during tableau*]—In the spring of 1834, Jason Lee and Cyrus Shepard, with their brides, set out "on their way to the Flathead Indians on the other side of the Rocky Mountains." On July 27, at Vancouver, in the valley of the Columbia, Lee preached the first Protestant sermon on the Pacific Coast. Continuing their journey they made a settlement on the shores of the Willamette and opened a school for the Indians. Later, when they began to migrate elsewhere, a school for the increasing number of whites was conducted. Lee formed a cattle company to import stock for the settlers. He prevented the first attempt to begin the manufacture of liquor in Oregon. He traveled widely, spreading information about Oregon and securing large funds for the work. He drafted a memorial to Congress, asking for the organization of Oregon as a territory. He went east and returned via steamer around Cape Horn with half a hundred new settlers. A string of mission stations, every one of which is now an important city, was established, and Lee's residence was the first dwelling built in Salem, now the capital of the state.

CURTAIN

CHOIR—"Blessed Assurance."

AMERICA—Another of these Western pioneers of the cross and a great highway builder, was Marcus Whitman, who took the first wagon over the Rocky Mountains, rode four thousand miles to save the Oregon country to the United States, and added three new stars to our flag. The Spirit of Missions will bring to our attention some of his greatest achievements.

SCENE 7

[MARCUS WHITMAN *preaching to a* GROUP OF INDIANS, *with* MRS. WHITMAN *at a portable organ.*]

MISSIONS [*during tableau*]—Marcus Whitman was trained for a physician, but became interested in missions and offered himself to the American Board of Missions, who sent him forth in 1836, to work among the Indians of the upper Columbia in the great Northwest. He was accompanied by his bride and three fellow missionaries, including H. H. Spalding and his bride. He insisted on taking a wagon, in spite of protests from every one, but after great difficulties he finally got it through, leaving the first wagon trail across the continent. A settlement was made at a place where Walla Walla is now located, a church and school were built and the Indians were taught in goodly numbers. At that time England desired this territory, known as Oregon, and the United States seemed indifferent. The Hudson Bay Company discouraged settlers from the East. Believing Oregon would be lost to the States, Whitman took his famous ride in midwinter, crossing icy rivers, sometimes lost in the snow, finally reaching Washington to urge Oregon's claim to the President. Daniel Webster objected that a wagon road could never be made across the Rockies, but Whitman was able to say he had made one himself. He returned with a large company of emigrants, but a few years later he and his wife, with twelve others, were brutally massacred by the Indians.

CURTAIN

CHOIR—"Faith Is the Victory."

AMERICA—It is said of Zacchæus that "he was small of stature," and that in his efforts to see Jesus in the crowd he had to climb up a tree. Our next story is about Sheldon

Jackson, who also was small of stature and of whom a newspaper reported that he was "short, bewhiskered, bespectacled; by inside measure a giant." This is a terse description of him in his prime.

SCENE 8

[SHELDON JACKSON, *with pack on his back, en route to a camp. Everything covered with white.*]

MISSIONS [*during tableau*]—Dedicated to the ministry at the age of four, it was first intended that Sheldon Jackson should go to the foreign field, but his health not permitting this, he went to Indian territory in the Southwest, then to Minnesota, and later became pioneer missionary superintendent of Presbyterian work in the entire Northwest, establishing many churches over an immense area. Then he heard the call of Alaska and went to see the field in 1877, returning to carry the news of Alaskan need from Atlantic to Pacific, making about nine hundred addresses in leading cities. In 1884 he became superintendent of missions in Alaska and carried on work there, under most difficult conditions. He traveled over ice fields, establishing schools and locating teachers in places where whales sported in the front yard in spring and polar bears prowled about in winter. He became "preacher, teacher, lawyer, doctor, nurse and business adviser of his people." He cleared ground, built houses and organized town governments. He was largely instrumental in securing territorial government and a school system for Alaska. He also made explorations of great value to the Government, and sent over twenty annual reports on education to Washington. His most important work was the introduction of reindeer into Alaska from Siberia, to provide the natives against famine. The sum of his journeys during his half century of service was about one million miles.

CURTAIN

CHOIR—"From Greenland's Icy Mountains."

AMERICA—The Protestant church has always stood for education, and schools have been established almost as soon as churches. When Dr. Jackson went to Alaska the first time, he felt that he dared not awaken the hopes of the Alaskans and leave them only with promises; he must take them a teacher.

SCENE 9

[MRS. MCFARLAND *as teacher of a* GROUP OF ALASKANS, *including men, women and children.*]

MISSIONS [*during tableau*]—He found a volunteer in Mrs. A. R. McFarland, who went with him to Fort Wragnell and remained there to teach in the school already opened by Philip McKay, a Christian native. For seven months she was the only Christian teacher in Alaska, and for five months longer she was alone at Fort Wrangell. She taught in an old dance house, with a native assistant, an interpreter, four Bibles, four hymnbooks, three Primers, thirteen First Readers and a wall chart as her equipment. She presided at a law-and-order meeting of natives; snatched tortured girls from the maddened heathen at a devil dance; conducted Sunday services and funerals; sheltered girls whose parents wanted to sell them, and constantly kept writing home for the help that was so long delayed. At last the longed-for minister arrived, and Mrs. McFarland could give herself to teaching, sewing schools and home visitation. She served twenty-two years.

CURTAIN

CHOIR—"O Jesus, I Have Promised."

AMERICA—No Christian workers are more deserving of honor than the Christian "Minutemen of the Frontier," who in the face of great obstacles steadily pushed the line of Christian occupation across the continent, planting churches and schools at every outpost.

SCENE 10

[Francis Higgins *preaching to a* Group of Lumberjacks, *with a barrel for a pulpit. Outdoor scene.*]

Missions [*during tableau*]—Francis E. Higgins was born in Toronto, Canada. Becoming a Christian while quite a young man, he organized a prayer-meeting group in a schoolhouse. Nine of the young men who attended these meetings became preachers. At the age of twenty-five he was licensed to preach and secured a church at Barnum, Minn. "It was at Barnum that he found himself and his beloved lumberjacks. Here he learned of the roaring 'river pigs' and the 'timber savages,' and his heart went out to them with a desire that was steadfast to the end. The unchurched foresters became his hearers, and beside the swift-flowing streams and in the low-built bunk houses he declared to them Christ's way of salvation. No more picturesque scene has ever flashed across the home mission screen than that of Francis Higgins, tramping with his pack from one camp to another, preaching with a barrel for a pulpit, dragging men from the saloon and the gambling table by physical force at times; no formal exhorter, but a real brother to men. He died at the age of forty-nine.

His life is typical of scores of others who have given themselves to lead men into the richer life.

CURTAIN

Choir—"America Befriend" [*tune, "America the Beautiful"*].

Highway Builders

O Lord, our God, Thy mighty hand
  Hath made our country free;
From all her broad and happy land
  May worship rise to Thee;
Fulfill the promise of her youth,
  Her liberty defend;
By law and order, love and truth,
  America befriend.

O suffer not her feet to stray,
  But guide her untaught might,
That she may walk in peaceful day,
  And lead the world in light.
Bring down the proud, lift up the poor,
  Unequal ways amend;
By justice, nation-wide and sure,
  America befriend.

Through all the waiting land proclaim
  The gospel of good will;
And may the joy of Jesus' name
  In every bosom thrill.
O'er hill and vale, from sea to sea,
  Thy holy reign extend;
By faith and hope and charity
  America befriend.   —*Author Unknown.*

A Cloud of Witnesses

A PAGEANT SHOWING THE WORK OF SOME PIONEER MISSIONARIES

CHARACTERS

THE SPIRIT OF MISSIONS.

SILAS................................Member of an Early Church

WILLIAM CAREY........................Missionary to India

ADONIRAM JUDSON......................Missionary to Burma

ROBERT MORRISON }
                                    Missionaries to China
WILLIAM MILNE   }

JOSEPH HARDY NEESIMA........Native Japanese Missionary

DAVID LIVINGSTONE....................Missionary to Africa

FIDELIA FISKE........................Missionary to Persia

KEITH FALCONER.......................Missionary to Arabia

WILLIAM M. THOMSON...................Missionary to Syria

CYRUS HAMLIN.........................Missionary to Turkey

TITUS COAN...........................Missionary to Hawaii

JOHN G. PATON...................Missionary to New Hebrides

JOHN WILLIAMS..................Missionary to Society Islands

DR. ALBERT SHELTON...................Missionary to Tibet

GROUP OF EARLY CHRISTIANS.

NATIVES of India, Burma, China, Japan, Africa, Persia, Arabia, Syria, Turkey, Hawaii, New Hebrides, Tibet and Society Islands.

COSTUMES

THE SPIRIT OF MISSIONS.

Modern dress or a bright robe.

111

EARLY CHRISTIANS.

　　See descriptions of costumes for other pageants.

THE MISSIONARIES.

　　Costumes of the nineteenth century.

THE NATIVES.

　　See section of "National Costumes."

ARRANGEMENTS

　　All scenes appear as tableaux, the characters remaining motionless while story is read. If a tarlatan curtain is hung over front of stage, the effect will be like oil paintings. Very little scenery is needed, but there may be a background of draperies or screens. Tall, artificial palms can be used effectively. The entire story is read from manuscript by the SPIRIT OF MISSIONS.

PAGEANT

　　CHOIR PRELUDE—"The Son of God Goes Forth to War." [*With cornet or orchestra.*]

　　MISSIONS—After the resurrection the disciples went into Galilee, unto the mountain where Jesus had appointed them. And He came and spake unto them, saying, "All authority hath been given unto me in heaven and on earth. Go ye therefore, and make disciples of all the nations, baptizing them in the name of the Father and of the Son and of the Holy Spirit; teaching them to observe all things whatsoever I commanded you. And lo, I am with you always, even unto the end of the world."

　　CHOIR—"Ye Christian Heralds." [*Three verses.*]

　　MISSIONS—In obeying this command, Saul of Tarsus, after the great Light had shined in his heart, journeyed for half a century through Palestine, Asia Minor and southern Europe, preaching, teaching, healing and building; wherefore he is today recorded as Paul, the first great missionary. [Hear ye his record and report, as written to some of the early churches:]

112

A Cloud of Witnesses

SCENE 1

[SILAS *stands reading from a scroll to a group of Christians who are seated.*]

MISSIONS [*during tableau*]—Brethren, my heart's desire and prayer to God for Israel is, that they might be saved. . . . For there is no difference between the Jew and the Greek; for the same Lord over all is rich unto all that call upon him. For whosoever shall call upon the name of the Lord shall be saved. How then shall they call on him in whom they have not believed? and how shall they believe in him of whom they have not heard? and how shall they hear without a preacher? And how shall they preach, except they be sent? as it is written, How beautiful are the feet of them that preach the gospel of peace, and bring glad tidings of good things? . . . For I will not dare to speak of any of those things which Christ hath not wrought by me, to make the Gentiles obedient, by word and deed, through many signs and wonders, by the power of the Spirit of God; so that from Jerusalem, and round about unto Illyricum, I have fully preached the gospel of Christ; not where Christ was named, lest I should build upon another man's foundation, but as it is written, To whom he was not spoken of, they shall see: and they that have not heard shall understand.

CURTAIN

CHOIR—"A Charge to Keep I Have." [*Four verses.*]

MISSIONS—Missionaries of the church are the world's greatest heroes. From the days of Paul to the days of John Wesley, they have endured "dungeon, fire and sword" that the gospel might live. And from the days of Wesley to the present day they have "kept the faith." This aggressive missionary work has been promoted by the Christians of all de-

8   113

nominations and has given to the world the most thrilling stories in literature, vibrant with life and heroism and help-fulness.] Tonight we are to visualize some of the world's greatest missionaries at their work. Let us remember how many hundreds there have been to go forth to distant lands, and that we can merely touch upon the lives of a few.

SCENE 2

[WILLIAM CAREY *is preaching to a group of Hindus. The scene may be an interior or an exterior, with branches of trees arranged at rear, right and left.* CAREY *is coatless.*]

MISSIONS [*during tableau*]—William Carey, the pioneer of modern missions, was an English shoemaker. Converted by a fellow apprentice, he became a Baptist preacher. One of his famous sayings is that his business was to preach the gospel, but he cobbled shoes to make a living. He became a missionary enthusiast, and at a ministers' meeting he preached a famous sermon, the theme of which was: "Expect great things from God; attempt great things for God." As a result of this sermon the first English missionary society was organized and Carey was sent to India as its first representa-tive.] Believing that a missionary should be self-supporting, he gave up his salary and obtained the superintendency of an indigo factory, in which he worked five years, preaching to his thousand laborers, itinerating among two hundred vil-lages, and translating the New Testament into the native language. He became so proficient in the Indian languages that he was made professor of them in Fort William College, and taught there for thirty years. He did great things, translating the Bible in whole or part into twenty-four of the Indian languages and dialects, and obtained, after many years' effort, the abolition of the terrible custom of burning widows on the funeral pyre of their dead husbands.

CURTAIN

CHOIR—"Jesus, I My Cross Have Taken."

SCENE 3

[ADONIRAM JUDSON *in a Burmese prison. He is on his knees beside a pile of straw on which is a copy of the Bible. A guard in Burmese costume stands by door at left. Dim light.*]

MISSIONS—Adoniram Judson and his wife, Ann, were leaders of the noble pioneer band of American missionaries. When only three years old he surprised his father one day by reading to him a chapter of the Bible. Judson was one of the Haystack Band at Williams College. They had formed the first foreign missionary society in America, and met at night to pray under a haystack. After his arrival in Burma he was asked concerning the prospects for converting the heathen and made his famous reply: "They are bright as the promises of God." During the war in which England conquered Burma, Judson was imprisoned by the natives and suffered horrible tortures, the effects of which remained with him for the remainder of his life. His precious translation of the Bible into the native language he sewed into a pillow, which was taken as a keepsake by a native Christian, and so it was preserved. It was six years before Judson won his first Burmese convert, but he lived to see the gospel firmly planted in Burma.

CURTAIN

CHOIR—"God Will Take Care of You."

SCENE 4

[ROBERT MORRISON *and* WILLIAM MILNE *are seated at a low table with several natives, translating the Bible. Use*

115

bamboo furniture, with a raffia porch shade in background.]

Missions [*during tableau*]—Robert Morrison, of Scotland, was the first Protestant missionary to China. On the way the shipowner asked him with a sneer, "Do you expect to make an impression on the idolatry of the great Chinese Empire?" His answer has become historic: "No, but I expect that God will." He faced four hundred million souls single-handed, and many of them were hostile. Morrison wore Chinese clothes and rarely ventured out at night. He studied incessantly and lived with such economy that at one time he could hardly walk across the room. Finally he secured a position as translator for the East India Company at $2,500 a year, and labored with more comfort for the rest of his life. Upon the arrival of William Milne, another missionary, they worked together on a translation of the Bible into Chinese, and made a great dictionary of the Chinese language, as well as a grammar. Morrison worked for seven years before he won his first convert, and he won only ten converts altogether, but in the twenty-seven years of his labors he laid a firm foundation upon which others might build.

CURTAIN

Choir—"Take My Life and Let It Be."

SCENE 5

[Joseph Hardy Neesima *seated upon the floor with eight Japanese students around him. Several scrolls with Japanese characters may be hung upon the walls.*]

Missions [*during tableau*]—Joseph Hardy Neesima was a Japanese boy, who at the age of fifteen, noticing that the idols did not eat the food placed before them, ceased to worship them. He found some books telling about the United States and Christianity, and longed to know more about both.

116

He earned his way across the ocean to America by waiting on table, being called "Joe." Arrived in America, he gained the interest of the ship's owner, a noble-hearted man named Alpheus Hardy, whose name he took for his middle name. Mr. Hardy put him through Phillips Academy and Amherst College. He visited Europe, and his reports became the foundation of Japan's present system of schools. Returning to Japan, he opened a Christian college, which started with only eight pupils, but became a great Christian institution. He was its president, made it a university, and in ten years had increased the eight students to 230. His life was one long, self-sacrificing effort for Japan, and when he died a building holding three thousand persons had to be erected for the funeral, and the procession was a mile and a half long.

CURTAIN

CHOIR—"I Am Thine, O Lord."

SCENE 6

[DAVID LIVINGSTONE *preaching to a group of Africans. He wears a white shirt and light trousers. Branches of trees or artificial palms will give an outdoor tropical effect.*]

MISSIONS [*during tableau*]—David Livingstone was the son of a poor Scotch weaver, who, after deciding to be a missionary, obtained a very practical training and went to Africa. There he toiled for the rest of his life, with the exception of a brief visit to England. He regarded exploration as the great work that must first be done, and his courageous and laborious travels opened up to missionary work a large part of the Dark Continent. Especially he unfolded the Zambezi country from ocean to ocean. He discovered many of the great African lakes, and described the regions around them. At one time he had a fight with a lion which bit through his arm bone. Most of his work was maintained by the sale of his books. On one of his journeys he read the Bible through four times. He gained a marvelous influence over the natives, who loved him as a brother, and he led large numbers of them to Christ. In his old age and when he was almost starving, Stanley was sent out to discover the discoverer, and did so in a moving fashion; but Livingstone refused to return to civilization. He grew more and more feeble and had to be carried by his black friends in a litter. At last he was found dead on his knees by his bed, having passed away in prayer for his beloved Africa. His heart was buried under a tree, and his body, having been embalmed, was carried laboriously on a nine months' journey to the coast, and now rests in Westminster Abbey.

CURTAIN

CHOIR—"He Leadeth Me."

SCENE 7

[FIDELIA FISKE *talking to a group of Persian girls. Persian tapestries may be hung upon the rear wall, if available.*]

MISSIONS [*during tableau*]—Miss Fidelia Fiske was a pioneer missionary to Persia. She found, in the city where she labored, only one woman who could read. She established a boarding school for girls, which did a wonderful work. The first Syriac word she learned was "daughters," and the next was "give," so that she could say, "Give me your daughters." Her pupils studied the Bible for three hours daily, and nearly all of them became Christians. A native chief, who was a very wicked character, brought his daughter to the school and was converted before he left the premises. All he could say was: "My great sins! My great Saviour!" The seminary enjoyed twelve revivals in its first nineteen years. Often the pupils would spend the entire night praying for their relatives. Miss Fiske made many journeys among the villages during her vacations, winning souls everywhere. At last her health gave out and she was compelled to return to America, where she died at the early age of forty-eight.

CURTAIN

CHOIR—"I Love to Tell the Story."

SCENE 8

[*Young* KEITH FALCONER *is preaching to a group of Arabians. Artificial palm trees may be used in the background.*]

MISSIONS [*during tableau*]—One of the young knights of missions was Ion Keith Falconer, of Scotland. He was brilliant in many directions, being president of the London Bicycle Club, a champion British runner, author of an article on shorthand for the Encyclopedia Britannica, and taking high university honors. He became interested in missions in Arabia and decided to found a medical mission there at his own expense, paying for the buildings and the assistants. He made many missionary tours in that terrible climate, preaching every day. Fevers seized upon him, one attack after the other, and he died at the age of forty; but the story of his heroism aroused great interest in his work, which has continued in much power ever since his untimely death.

CURTAIN

CHOIR—"Have Thine Own Way, Lord."

SCENE 9

[WILLIAM M. THOMSON *as teacher of a class of Syrian boys.*]

MISSIONS [*during tableau*]—William McClure Thomson, a native of Ohio, went out in 1833, and after many thrilling adventures and sorrows reached Syria, where he helped open the first boarding school for boys in the Turkish Empire. It was during a civil war in Syria, as Dr. Thomson started on a tour to Jaffa, that he was arrested as a spy and was detained forty days. After the fall of Jerusalem he was released, but found his wife critically ill from shock during the terrors of the siege, and she lived but a short time. His forty-three years of ministry were crowded with service, including the publication of "The Land and the Book," a marvelous story of Palestine and the Bible.

CURTAIN

CHOIR—"'Tis So Sweet to Trust in Jesus."

SCENE 10

[CYRUS HAMLIN *standing before a class of Turkish students.*]

MISSIONS [*during tableau*]—Cyrus Hamlin was a poor boy in New England, but he was full of resources and became a glorious missionary in Turkey. He was a genuine Yankee, able to turn his hand to anything. He ran a lathe, made chemical and physical apparatus, and started workshops to manufacture clothing for his pupils. He manufactured stove pipes and stoves. During the Crimean War he set up an immense bakery, supplying the British soldiers with fourteen thousand pounds of bread a day. His great work was the founding of Robert College, that splendid educational institution in Constantinople. One of his splendid statements was: "Let me fail in trying to do something, rather than to sit still and do nothing."

CURTAIN

CHOIR—"Work, for the Night Is Coming."

SCENE 11

[TITUS COAN *preaching to a group of Hawaiians. If possible, arrange this as an outdoor scene, with tall palms in rear.*]

MISSIONS [*during tableau*]—Titus Coan was the son of a New England farmer, who, after being licensed to preach, was sent to Patagonia as a missionary, accompanied by Rev. Mr. Arms. For four months they made an earnest, but unsuccessful, attempt to communicate with the ferocious nomads. The savages threatened them with death, and it was only by stratagem that they made their escape and returned to America. Seven months later Mr. Coan embarked with his bride for Honolulu, the journey taking six months around Cape Horn. Other missionaries in Hawaii welcomed them gladly, and they established a home on the beautiful bay of Hilo. Within three months Mr. Coan began to speak in the native language, and traveled continually, preaching and also ministering to the sick. Within two years after his arrival 15,000 people had become Christians. On one Sunday afternoon 1,705 men, women and children were baptized, and about 2,400 communicants partook of the Lord's Supper. During his ministry of forty-eight years he baptized more than 12,000 persons.

CURTAIN

CHOIR—"O Jesus, I Have Promised."

SCENE 12

[JOHN G. PATON *preaching to a group of natives in the New Hebrides, with a setting similar to last scene.*]

MISSIONS [*during tableau*]—John G. Paton was a native of Scotland, who spent ten years as a worker in the Glasgow

121

city mission before leaving with his bride for the New Hebrides. They established a home on the Island of Tanna, where they lived for three years. The natives were in the lowest depths of heathenism and the missionaries were in constant danger. After the death of his wife and infant son he went to another station on the island. After visits in Australia and Scotland, presenting the cause of missions, he returned to the islands with a new bride and settled on Aniwa, where they were well received because of threats made by an old chief from Tanna. Mr. Paton translated the Bible into the Aniwa language and made many conversions.

CURTAIN

CHOIR—"O Jesus, I Have Promised."

SCENE 13

[JOHN WILLIAMS *and group of natives on the Society Islands, building a house with bamboo—small limbs from your native trees. There should be a tropical background.*]

MISSIONS [*during tableau*]—John Williams was a wild youth in London, who was converted by a passing invitation to church given him by a good woman. At the age of twenty he became a missionary to the Society Islands in the Southern Pacific, and could preach in the native language within ten months, an achievement usually requiring three years. He taught the natives how to build houses, and they constructed an amazing church, with chandeliers made by Williams and cocoanut shells for lamps. He obtained a colored plaster from the coral and also made all kinds of furniture. He built boats without nails. He constructed a sugar mill. He made machinery to manufacture rope. He established schools, reduced the language to writing, and drew up a code of laws. He built a ship sixty feet long in which he explored the South

122

Seas, everywhere planting the seeds of Christianity. He went as far as the New Hebrides, where he was murdered by some natives, who confused him with some of the cruel white traders who had wronged them.

CURTAIN

CHOIR—"Take the Name of Jesus with You."

SCENE 14

[DR. ALBERT SHELTON *in hospital scene with natives of Tibet.*]

MISSIONS [*during tableau*]—In Tibet and other provinces of western China it is estimated that there are twelve million non-Christians, with no missionaries, for these lands are practically closed even to this day. The most promising approach to Tibet has been made through the work of the medical missionary. In 1903, Dr. Albert Shelton, representing the Disciples of Christ, went to the Himalaya country, and five years later he opened a station and hospital in Batang, near the border of Tibet. In his first serious case he saved the life of a native whose head had been crushed. The gratitude of the patient and his parents sounded a trumpet for the gospel. His increasing popularity brought him into conflict with the monks, for they reaped a rich harvest from the sale of charm boxes warranted to protect the wearer from injury. After a year of work at home, on returning to Tibet, Dr. Shelton was shot by a bandit. In accord with the policy of China to discourage travel and exploration, Lhasa, the capital of Tibet, is a city of mystery.

CURTAIN

CHOIR—"Jesus Calls Us o'er the Tumult."

MISSIONS—"Seeing we are encompassed with so great a cloud of witnesses, let us lay aside every weight, and the sin which doth so easily beset us, and let us run with patience the race that is set before us, looking unto Jesus, the captain of our faith, who, for the joy that was set before him endured the cross, despising the shame, and is set down at the right hand of the throne of God."

Go to the lands afar,
  Where the changeless winter reigns:
Night hath her empires there,
The night of deep despair;
Go, bid the Morning Star
  Rise o'er those snowy plains.

Go, love's soft dew to shower
  On the far-off southern isles:
Though darkness hath her hour,
Truth is a mightier power:
Go, bid the lily flower
  And the rose of Sharon smile.

Go where its glittering wave
  The spreading Ganges pours:
No hidden power to save
Those earthborn waters have;
O purer streamlets wave
  Zion's thrice-hallowed shores.

Go where o'er golden sands
  The streams of Africa glide:
Bear to those distant lands
The Saviour's sweet commands;
Firm, firm His purpose stands,
  "Lo, I am by thy side!"

Wide is the glorious field.
  Throughout the world go forth
The Spirit's sword to wield,
To bear the Spirit's shield,
Till every nation yield,
  And blessings crown the earth.
                                    —*Author Unknown.*

CHOIR—"We've a Story to Tell to the Nations."

SCENE 15

[*All characters of pageant grouped in tiers, facing rear wall, upon which hangs a gilded cross, to which the characters have their arms extended.*]

MISSIONS [*during tableau*]—"I saw a new heaven and a new earth, for the first heaven and the first earth are passed away, and I saw the Holy City, New Jerusalem, coming down out of heaven from God. And I heard a great voice out of the throne, saying, Behold the tabernacle of God is with men, and he shall dwell with them and they shall be his people."

CURTAIN

CHOIR [*during tableau*]—"All Hail the Power of Jesus' Name."

Defenders of the Faith*

A PAGEANT SHOWING THE EARLY LEADERS OF THE CHURCH

CHARACTERS

READERS

SPIRIT OF RELIGION.   THE RECORDER MATTHEW.
SPIRIT OF HISTORY.   THE RECORDER LUKE.

TABLEAUX

PETER ⎫
JAMES ⎬ _____Apostles of Jesus
JOHN ⎭
ANANIAS_____The High Priest
CLETUS AND TIMON_____Roman Guards
MEMBERS OF THE SANHEDRIN.
STEPHEN_____First Christian Martyr
PAUL_____The First Great Missionary
SILAS_____One of His Companions
JONAS_____A Philippian Jailer
NERO_____Emperor of Rome
COMPANY OF ROMAN SOLDIERS.
POLYCARP_____Bishop of Smyrna
ORIGEN_____A Great Writer
SEBASTIAN _____A Soldier-Martyr

---

* Information regarding the later church leaders, beginning with Peter Waldo, taken from "Missionary Milestones," by Margaret R. Seebach, and used by permission of the Council of Women for Home Missions.

PETER WALDO............................A French Reformer
JOHN WYCLIFFE..............Author of the English Bible
JOHN HUSS..............Bohemian Reformer and Martyr
JEROME SAVONAROLA......Italian Reformer and Martyr
MARTIN LUTHER..................Father of the Reformation
PREACHER.
ULRICH ZWINGLI..........................A Swiss Reformer
COMPANY OF SWISS SOLDIERS.
JOHN CALVIN....................French-Swiss Reformer
JACQUES LEFEVRE......................A French Reformer
WILLIAM TYNDALE......Leader of English Reformation
THOMAS CRANMER........................English Martyr
JOHN KNOX........................Scotch Reformer
JOHN WESLEY........................English Reformer
EXECUTIONERS.
PRISONERS.
JEWS.
GROUP OF EARLY CHRISTIANS.
NERO'S ATTENDANTS.
GROUP OF WALDENSIANS.
CITIZENS OF ENGLAND.
CITIZENS OF FLORENCE.
CITIZENS OF PARIS.
CITIZENS OF GENEVA.
GROUP OF HOLLANDERS.
GROUP OF SCOTCHMEN.

COSTUMES

BIBLE CHARACTERS.

Flowing robes of white or striped material, made from sheets or
flannel nightgowns. Six-foot shoulder scarfs, one yard wide, made
from bright cloth or striped material. Bare legs, with sandals.
Turbans of bright cloth. STEPHEN and PETER have short, gray
beards, the others dark brown.

ANANIAS.

Robe of white, reaching to ankles. Over this is a cloak of soft-
blue material (outing flannel), with elbow-length sleeves and reaching to knees. Over this is a short skirt of deep lace. Square, white

"bib" with twelve criss-crosses made with colored crayons. White turban with square of gold paper in front.

ROMAN CHARACTERS.

Knee-length tunic of tan and a bright girdle. Cape hanging from back of shoulders. Brown socks with sandal strings laced over them. Helmet made from a sheet of gold paper pinned around the head, and two ends making "wings" at each side.

NERO.

Robe of rich material; no head covering.

POLYCARP.

Costume like Bible Characters, without turban.

MEDIEVAL CHURCH LEADERS AND CITIZENS.

Study historical pictures, most of which reveal smocklike garments with small hats.

SWISS SOLDIERS.

Tunics of brown cloth and helmets of brown paper.

EARLY CHRISTIANS.

Men as described above; women with flowing robes.

RELIGION AND HISTORY.

Flowing robes of bright colors.

(Details of costumes will not be closely observed because of the many characters participating in the group scenes.)

ARRANGEMENTS

The entire story is read from manuscripts attached to scrolls. All four READERS and choir leader should have copies of complete manuscript.

With the exception of Scene 1, all scenes are to appear as tableaux, the characters remaining motionless while story is read. If a tarlatan curtain is hung over the front of the stage, the effect will be like oil paintings. It is not really necessary.

Very little scenery is needed, but there may be a background of draperies or painted sets. Folding screens may be used at each end to make entrances. Branches of trees, chairs, altars, temple steps, etc., are added as designated.

1. Matthew's Record.
2. The Apostles Are Threatened.
3. The First Christian Martyr.
4. Paul the Persecutor.
5. Paul in Prison.
6. James Becomes a Martyr.
7. The Persecutions of Nero.
8. The Persecutions of Domitian.
9. Polycarp Becomes a Martyr.
10. Origen Spreads the Gospel.
11. Sebastian Becomes a Martyr.
12. Waldo Leads a Reform in France.
13. Wycliffe and the English Bible.
14. Huss, of Bohemia, Is a Martyr.
15. Savonarola Preaches a Reform.
16. Luther Revolts Against Rome.
17. Massacre of the Huguenots.
18. The Hollanders Are Persecuted.
19. Zwingli, of Switzerland, Is a Martyr.
20. Calvin Becomes a Reformer.
21. Lefevre Promotes Reform in France.
22. Tyndale and His Bible Attacked.
23. Cranmer Is a Martyr in England.
24. John Knox Leads the Scotchmen.
25. Wesley, Flaming Evangel.

PAGEANT

CHOIR—"Ancient of Days." [*Used as a processional.*]

RELIGION—One night, more than nineteen hundred years ago, in the tiny hamlet of Bethlehem, in Judea, a remote province of the Roman Empire, Jesus of Nazareth was born. Announced as the Messiah of Israel, He lived, preached, gathered disciples, and then died on the cross. Some of His commands, as recorded by Matthew, were the challenge for many thousands to obey. Hear Matthew's record:

SCENE 1

[MATTHEW *reading from a scroll to group of people.*]

MATTHEW—"Behold, I send you forth as sheep in the midst of wolves: be ye therefore wise as serpents, and harmless as doves. But beware of men: for they will deliver you up to the councils, and they will scourge you in their synagogues; And ye shall be brought before governors and kings for my sake, . . . But when they deliver you up, take no thought how or what ye shall speak: for it shall be given you in that same hour what ye shall speak. For it is not ye that speak, but the Spirit of your Father which speaketh in you. . . . And ye shall be hated of all men for my name's sake: but he that endureth to the end shall be saved. . . . Whosoever therefore shall confess me before men, him will I confess also before my Father which is in heaven. . . . Go ye therefore, and teach all nations, baptizing them in the name of the Father, and of the Son, and of the Holy Ghost: Teaching them to observe all things whatsoever I have commanded you: and, lo, I am with you alway, even unto the end of the world."

CHOIR—"Joy to the World." [*One verse.*]

LUKE [*at one side of platform, out in front*]—"And by the hands of the apostles were many signs and wonders wrought among the people; . . . And believers were the more added to the Lord, multitudes both of men and women. Insomuch that they brought forth the sick into the streets, and laid them on beds and couches, that at the least the shadow of Peter passing by might overshadow some of them. There came also a multitude out of the cities round about unto Jerusalem, bringing sick folks, and them which were vexed with unclean spirits: and they were healed every one. Then the high priest rose up, and all they that were with him, . . . and were filled with indignation, And laid their

131

hands on the apostles, and put them in the common prison. But the angel of the Lord by night opened the doors, and brought them forth, and said, Go, stand and speak in the temple to the people all the words of this life. . . . Now when the high priest and all they that were with him heard these things, they had the apostles brought unto them without violence, for they feared the people."

SCENE 2

[PETER, JAMES *and* JOHN *before* ANANIAS *and* MEMBERS OF THE SANHEDRIN, *with two* GUARDS *on either side.* ANANIAS *sits upon an elevated chair and* MEMBERS OF THE SANHEDRIN *on each side.*]

LUKE [*during tableau*]—"And when they had brought them, they set them before the council: and the high priest asked them, Saying, Did not we straitly command you that ye should not teach in this name? and, behold, ye have filled Jerusalem with your doctrine, and intend to bring this man's blood upon us. Then Peter answering, said, We ought to obey God rather than men. The God of our fathers raised up Jesus, whom ye slew and hanged on a tree. Him hath God exalted with his right hand to be a Prince and a Saviour, for to give repentance to Israel, and forgiveness of sins. And we are his witnesses of these things; and so is also the Holy Ghost, whom God hath given to them that obey him. When they heard that, they were cut to the heart, and took counsel to slay them. And when they had called the apostles, and beaten them, they commanded that they should not speak in the name of Jesus, and let them go. And they departed from the council, rejoicing that they were counted worthy to suffer shame for his name. And daily in the temple, and in every house, they ceased not to teach and preach Jesus Christ."

CURTAIN

CHOIR—"Alas! and Did My Saviour Bleed?" [*One verse.*]

LUKE—"And Stephen, full of faith and power, did great wonders and miracles among the people. Then there arose certain of the synagogue, disputing with Stephen. But they were not able to resist the wisdom and the spirit by which he spake. Then they stirred up the people, and the elders, and the scribes, and came upon him and brought him to the council, and set up false witnesses, which said, This man ceaseth not to speak blasphemous words against this holy place, and the law; for we have heard him say that this Jesus of Nazareth shall destroy this place, and shall change the customs which Moses delivered us. And all that sat in the council, looking stedfastly on him, saw his face as it had been the face of an angel. Then said the high priest, Are these things so? And he said, Ye stiffnecked and uncircumcised in heart and ears, ye do always resist the Holy Ghost: as your fathers did, so do ye. Which of the prophets have not your fathers persecuted? and they have slain them which shewed before of the coming of the Just One, of whom ye have now become the betrayers and murderers. And when they heard these things, they were cut to the heart, and gnashed on him with their teeth. But he, being full of the Holy Ghost, looked up stedfastly into heaven and said, Behold, I see the Son of man standing on the right hand of God. Then they cried with a loud voice and stopped their ears, and ran upon him."

SCENE 3

[*A group of men are stoning* STEPHEN, *who is on his knees with face and arms uplifted. Inflated paper bags may be used for stones.*]

LUKE [*during tableau*]—"And they cast him out of the city, and stoned him, calling upon God and saying, Lord Jesus, receive my spirit. And he kneeled down and cried with a loud voice, Lord, lay not this sin to their charge. And when he had said this, he fell asleep."

CURTAIN

CHOIR—"Holy Spirit, Faithful Guide." [*One verse.*]

SCENE 4

[GROUP OF EARLY CHRISTIANS *kneeling and standing, with arms uplifted to protect themselves from a lash which* PAUL *holds in his upraised hand.* ROMAN SOLDIERS *with* PAUL.]

LUKE [*during tableau*]—"And at that time there was a great persecution against the church which was at Jerusalem and they were all scattered abroad, throughout the regions of Judæa and Samaria, except the apostles. And a Pharisee from Tarsus, named Saul, made havoc of the church, entering into every house, and hailing men and women committed them to prison."

CURTAIN

CHOIR—" 'Tis So Sweet to Trust in Jesus." [*One verse.*]

RELIGION—Not long after, the "great Light" opened the blinded eyes and closed heart of this same persecutor, and, as a herald of the cross, he went through cities and villages, preaching the glad tidings, whence he also suffered the persecutions which he aforetime had inflicted. Once, in Philippi, he and his companion, Silas, were arrested and cast into prison.

SCENE 5

[*In the prison. Dim light from lantern overhead.* JONAS *is kneeling before* PAUL *and* SILAS. PRISONERS *in rear.*]

LUKE [*during tableau*]—"And at midnight Paul and Silas prayed, and sang praises unto God, and the prisoners heard them. And suddenly there was a great earthquake, so that the foundations of the prison were shaken and immediately all the doors were opened, and every one's bands were unloosed. And the keeper of the prison came trembling and fell down before Paul and Silas, crying, Sirs, what must I do to be saved? And they said, Believe on the Lord Jesus Christ, and thou shalt be saved, and thy house. And they spake unto him the word of the Lord, and to all that were in the house. And he took them and washed their wounds and was baptized."

CURTAIN

CHOIR—"Blessed Assurance." [*One verse.*]

RELIGION—James, the Lord's brother, was surnamed "The Just" by his countrymen. It is said that he was a Nazarite from birth, abstaining from wine and animal food, and observing all standards of the law. Was early recognized as bishop of Jerusalem.

SCENE 6

[*In front of a temple balcony.* JAMES *is kneeling, face uplifted, and arms raised to protect himself from stones being hurled at him by enraged Jews, including* ANANIAS.]

RELIGION [*during tableau*]—Ananias, the high priest, and the scribes and Pharisees, taking advantage of the interim between the death of Festus and the new Roman governor, assembled the council and commanded James to proclaim from one of the galleries of the temple that Jesus was not the Messiah, in order to restrain the people who were embracing Christianity in large numbers. But James cried out that Jesus was the Son of God and Judge of the world. His enraged enemies hurled him to the ground and then stoned him, until a charitable fuller ended his sufferings with a club while he was on his knees praying, "Father, forgive them; they know not what they do." Shortly afterward the fatal siege of Jerusalem began. The Jews felt that had James lived he might have averted the destruction of the city and deemed it a judgment on them for the murder of this Christian.

CURTAIN

CHOIR—"I Know Whom I Have Believed." [*One verse.*]

HISTORY—Meanwhile, out from Judea the apostles have gone to the towns of Asia Minor, to Greece, to Egypt and to Italy, preaching the new gospel. Then suddenly pagan Rome turns against the new religion and persecutions begin.

SCENE 7

[*Balcony at rear, from which* NERO *and his* ATTENDANTS *behold five or six posts, to which* EARLY CHRISTIANS *are bound.* EXECUTIONERS, *garbed in old clothes, have torches—electric-light bulbs covered with red paper—as if ready to burn the* CHRISTIANS.]

RELIGION [*during tableau*]—It was in the tenth year of the reign of the brutal Nero that the so-called great fire laid more than half of Rome in ashes. It was rumored that Nero had ordered the conflagration to be lighted, and that from the roof of his palace he enjoyed the spectacle, amusing himself by playing his fiddle. Nero did everything in his power to discredit the rumor and finally accused the Christians. The persecution that followed was one of the most cruel recorded in the history of the church. Many victims were covered with pitch and burned at night, to serve as torches in the imperial gardens. Tradition says that the apostles Peter and Paul were victims of this persecution.

CURTAIN

CHOIR—"O for a Faith that Will Not Shrink." [*Two verses.*]

HISTORY—Nero was followed by emperors whose total reigns covered about twenty years, including ten years of constructive leadership under Vespasian and two years under Titus, who won the title "The Delight of Mankind" because of his benevolence and kindness.

SCENE 8

[*A street where a group of* CHRISTIANS *are being arrested by a company of* ROMAN SOLDIERS *with raised daggers and spears. The* CHRISTIANS *have arms raised in protection.*]

RELIGION [*during tableau*]—Domitian's reign of fifteen years was in exact contrast to that of his brother, Titus. It was one succession of extravagances, tyrannies and murders. He instituted what is known in church history as the "second persecution of the Christians," on the charge of atheism, because they refused to worship the statues of himself which he had set up. Many thousands were slain in Rome and throughout Italy. The apostle John was banished to the Isle of Patmos.

CURTAIN

CHOIR—" 'Tis by the Faith of Joys to Come." [*First and third verses.*]

HISTORY—Domitian was followed by five good emperors —Nerva, Trajan, Hadrian, Antoninus and Marcus Aurelius. But during the reign of Marcus Aurelius there were wars with the hostile Parthians, and the returning soldiers brought with them the Asiatic plague, which swept off vast numbers, especially in Italy, where entire cities and districts were depopulated. In the general distress and panic the superstitious people were led to believe that it was the new sect of Christians that had called down upon the nation the anger of the gods, and Aurelius permitted a fearful persecution to be instituted against them.

SCENE 9

[*A street or court where* POLYCARP *is standing beside a stake, surrounded by a* COMPANY OF SOLDIERS.]

RELIGION [*during tableau*]—During this persecution many thousands were beheaded or thrown to the wild beasts. The tortures of the victims, endured without flinching, almost surpasses belief. The famous martyr, Polycarp, bishop of Smyrna, who was nearly ninety years old, was among the victims. When he was brought forth to worship the statue of Tiberius, a voice seemed to urge him, saying, "Be strong, Polycarp, and show thyself a man," so he refused to bow before the image.

"Reproach Christ and I will set thee at liberty," urged the proconsul.

But Polycarp stood unflinchingly and replied, "Eighty and six years have I served Him and He has done me nothing but good; how, then, can I blaspheme Him, my Lord and Saviour? Hear me declare with all boldness, I am a Christian."

"I will cause thee to be consumed with fire if thou wilt not repent," threatened the proconsul.

"Thou threatenest me with fire which burneth for an hour and then is extinguished, but art ignorant of the fire of consuming judgment and of eternal punishment, reserved for the ungodly. Bring forth what thou wilt."

"Burn him! burn him! burn him!" cried the frenzied mob.

The fagots were piled around him and Polycarp lifted his voice in prayer: "I give Thee thanks, my Father, that Thou hast counted me worthy of this day and this hour, that

I should have a part in the number of Thy martyrs, in the cup of Thy Christ, to the resurrection of eternal life."

CURTAIN

HISTORY—After the flames had consumed his body the Christians of Smyrna gathered his bones and buried them, and on the hill, just outside the city today, there is a tomb which is said to be that of Polycarp.

CHOIR—"Jesus, Lover of My Soul." [*One verse.*]

HISTORY—Other famous leaders who suffered martyrdom about the same time as Polycarp were Papias and Justin. Papias was bishop of Hierapolis, and wrote a book entitled "Explanation of the Lord's Discourses," in which he states that he made it a point to inquire of the church elders the exact words of Jesus. Justin traveled in a philosopher's robe, seeking to win men to Christ. He wrote a "Defense of Christianity," addressed to the emperor, but was beheaded in Rome. The Emperor Aurelius was followed by the twelve-year reign of the insane tyrant Commodus, and then nearly a century under the "Barrack Emperors," who were elected by the army. Then followed eighteen years under Septimus Severus, who instituted a persecution of the Christians which was most severe in Egypt and North Africa, where many martyrs were daily burned, crucified or beheaded. The next persecution took place during the brief administration of Maximin, when many prominent Christian leaders were put to death, and he was followed by brief reigns under Gordian and Philip.

SCENE 10

[ORIGEN *and a dozen or more* EARLY CHRISTIANS (*men*) *seated around table, writing.*]

RELIGION [*during tableau*]—The next emperor, Decius, resolutely determined to exterminate Christianity and multitudes perished under the most cruel tortures. One of the victims was Origen, the most learned man of the ancient church. He was a great traveler and a voluminous writer, employing at times as many as twenty copyists. Two-thirds of the New Testament is quoted in his writings. He lived in Alexandria, where his father, Leonidas, also suffered martyrdom.

CURTAIN

CHOIR—"How Firm a Foundation." [*One verse.*]

HISTORY—It was under the reign of Diocletian that the government finally became an unveiled and absolute monarchy. During his reign the tenth, the last and severest of the persecutions of the church took place. By an imperial decree the churches of the Christians were ordered to be torn down and they themselves were outlawed.

SCENE 11

[*Outdoor scene, with* SEBASTIAN *bound to a tree and several* ROMAN SOLDIERS *aiming at him with bow and arrow.*]

RELIGION [*during tableau*]—For ten years the fugitives were hunted in forest and cave, and the poor victims put to death by every torture that ingenius cruelty could devise. But nothing could shake the constancy of their faith and multitudes came to join with them. One of the famous martyrs of this period was Sebastian, a Roman soldier. When it was discovered that he was a Christian he was first bound to a tree, shot with arrows, and then beaten to death.

CURTAIN

CHOIR—"Soldiers of Christ, Arise." [*Two verses.*]

HISTORY—It was during the later persecutions that the Christians sought refuge in the catacombs, those vast subterranean chambers under the city of Rome. Here they hope-

140

fully buried their dead, and on the walls sketched rude symbols of their confident faith. It was in the darkness of these abodes that Christian art had its beginnings.

RELIGION—Among the outstanding witnesses for Christ and the church during this period were Eusebius, the "father of church history"; John Chrysostom, a matchless orator, who became known as the "golden mouthed," and preached to great multitudes, but, being a reformer, he was banished and died in exile; Jerome, who translated the Bible into the Latin language, called the Vulgate, which today is the authorized Bible of the Roman Catholic Church; and Augustine, in North Africa, the greatest thinker of the early church and who did more than any other to mold the doctrines of the church of the Middle Ages.

HISTORY—After ruling for twenty-one years and then becoming weary of the affairs of state, Diocletian abdicated the throne and retired to a country estate. After several years of strife, Constantine became sole ruler of the Roman world, and, after being converted, he made Christianity the state religion.

CHOIR—"Onward, Christian Soldiers." [*One verse.*]

HISTORY—We can not tell the exact date at which the Bishops of Rome began to claim supremacy over all other Christian authorities. At first the Bishop or Pope was merely the spiritual head of the church in the capital of the empire, but, as time passed, more and more power was attributed to him, until in the chaos that followed the fall of Rome the church was the only power strong enough to curb the barbarians who ruled the empire and to protect the people from violence. Naturally the Popes came to the position of dictators, whom warriors and kings obeyed. This would have been a frightfully dangerous power, even in the hands of righteous men, but the priesthood had degenerated into such moral conditions that words can not picture it. Acknowledging no higher law, they became a "law unto themselves," with the usual results of laxity and extortion.

RELIGION—In return for all this, they gave the people nothing but the routine performance of liturgical forms. Preaching amounted to little but the rehearsing of traditions and legends of the saints, often grotesque and nonsensical. Pictures and images were placed in the churches to help the ignorant laity in their devotions; the most gross idolatry was often the result. The people were taught that God could not be approached, even through His Son, without intervention of the virgin Mary or of some one of the many saints of the Roman Church. Penance, or the mortifying of the flesh, was substituted for penitence of the heart. Meanwhile the priests themselves often set their people the example of a life given over to excess of every kind. Who will deny that there was cause for protest? And protest had not been lacking for several centuries.

HISTORY—One of the first means of papal persecutions was the Inquisition, or spiritual court of the church. Under it every one was required to inform against heretics. Any one suspected was liable to torture, without knowing the name of his accuser. The proceedings were very secret and the victims were usually burned alive in the public square. It was used with terrible effect in Spain, France, Germany, Portugal, Italy and the Netherlands to extend the power of the papacy.

SCENE 12

[WALDO *is preaching to a group of people.*]

RELIGION [*during tableau*]—One of the first groups to make an organized protest against the religious conditions were the Waldenses, "the Israelites of the Alps." Peter Waldo, a merchant of Lyons in France, employed priests to translate parts of the Bible for him. He was so impressed by the truths he learned that he began to repeat passages of Scripture to others and to speak about the wrongs he saw under the guise of religion. His followers also preached throughout southern Europe until they were excommunicated by the Church of Rome and driven to shelter in the Alpine valleys. For three centuries and more they were the object of bitter persecutions, yet they managed to send abroad copies of the Scriptures translated into the popular tongue, by traveling as peddlers, with the precious books concealed in rolls of merchandise. Many of them also were able to recite whole Gospels from memory. A remnant of the Waldensian Church still survives in northern Italy.

CURTAIN

CHOIR—"God Will Take Care of You." [*One verse.*]

SCENE 13

[WYCLIFFE *seated at a table, writing. Two friends (any of* CITIZENS) *may also be seated with him, if desired.*]

RELIGION [*during tableau*]—John Wycliffe, "The Morning Star of the Reformation," was an Oxford scholar, rector of Lutterworth, chaplain and adviser to the king. He denied the civil authority of the pope, insisted that the highest service of the clergy was to preach the Word of God to the people, and that the one rule of faith and life is found in the Scriptures. He was pronounced a heretic, and, being forbidden to preach, he gave himself to making the first translation of the Bible into English. So dreadful a heresy was this considered that thirty years after his death the reading of the English Bible was forbidden to the people "upon pain of forfeiture of land, stock, life and goods from their heirs forever." Some years later, by order of the Council of Constance, his bones were disinterred and burned and the ashes cast into the river Swift. In the words of Fuller, "They were carried thence into Avon, from the Avon into Severn, from Severn into the narrow seas, and thence into the main ocean, from whence they were spread the world over, thus being the emblem of his doctrine."

CURTAIN

CHOIR—"Wonderful Words of Life." [*One verse.*]

SCENE 14

[*Outdoor scene, where* HUSS *is bound to a post, surrounded by brush ready to be lighted by* EXECUTIONERS *with torches. If desired, a preaching scene may be substituted.*]

RELIGION [*during tableau*]—At Prague, in Bohemia, another preacher and university professor, John Huss, took up the views of Wycliffe and translated them into the language of his people, besides writing protests of his own against the papacy. Excommunicated and driven from Prague, he preached in the fields and woods to all who came to hear him. "It is better," he declared, "to die well than to live badly. Truth is the last conqueror." Summoned before the Council of Constance, he was imprisoned for several months in vile dungeons and assailed by false witnesses. When he was brought forth on July 6, 1415, and given a final opportunity to retract, he declared himself willing to retract whatever words of his could be proved false by Scripture, but nothing else, and, as no one was able to meet his challenge, he declared he would be burned a thousand times rather than abjure his teachings. When the fagots around him were lighted he prayed, "Lord Jesus Christ, I will bear patiently and humbly this horrible, cruel death for the sake of the gospel and the preaching of Thy Word."

CURTAIN

CHOIR—"My Faith Looks Up to Thee." [*Three verses.*]

HISTORY—The evangelical church in Bohemia and Moravia was a survival of the teachings of John Huss and these "Bohemian Brethren." Balthasar Hubmaier, their great preacher of the Reformation, was driven from Austria and took refuge in Moravia, where he built up a strong church. But Austria followed him with a charge of "rebellion against the government," in addition to the charge of heresy, and after some months of imprisonment he was burned at Vienna. His devoted wife was three days later thrown into the Danube, with a great stone tied around her neck. Jerome, of Prague, another Bohemian reformer and companion of Huss, was burned at the stake and his ashes thrown into the Rhine.

SCENE 15

[*The public square in Florence, where* SAVONAROLA *is preaching and people are casting trinkets into a bonfire—a light bulb covered with red paper and brush.*]

RELIGION [*during tableau*]—A still more dramatic protest was that of Savonarola, in Italy. Like one of the ancient prophets, he shook the city of Florence by his eloquence, denouncing the sins of the people and the iniquities of the church. "I preach the regeneration of the church," he said, "taking the Scriptures as my whole guide." The pope tried to bribe him into silence by the offer of a cardinalate, but he declared that he desired only the honor which God gives to His saints. Moved as by an angel's voice, the gay and luxurious citizens brought their trinkets, mirrors, dice, cosmetics and other vanities and cast them into a great bonfire in the public square. Savonarola proclaimed that henceforth Jesus Christ, and He alone, was King over Florence. More and more bitter grew his denunciations of Rome. Then an ordeal by fire was proposed, to settle the dispute, but its fiasco set the fickle populace to mob their former idol and he was tortured and finally executed.

CURTAIN

CHOIR—"Beneath the Cross of Jesus." [*Two verses.*]

HISTORY—Not only scholars, but the unlettered and humble could see by this time the frightful abuses wrought in the name of the Roman Church. Every rank of society was ready for revolt against its yoke of bondage, if only a leader could be found. The time was ripe for the man of God's choosing. The great leader of the Reformation was Martin, son of Hans Luther, a humble miner in the German village of Eisleben. After struggling for his education, including a course at the university, he entered the monastery at Erfurt. Thinking that he would win salvation from sin by his own sufferings, he indulged in various forms of torture, but could find no peace. Then he began to read the Scriptures and immediately found comfort and encouragement. When he was appointed instructor in the University of Wittenberg he studied the Scriptures with great earnestness and learned that we are saved by faith in Jesus Christ. Upon preaching this doctrine he came into conflict with the pope and the Roman Church. He was disgusted by the sale of indulgences, or written pardons for sin, which the pope was selling to raise funds to complete the building of St. Peter's Church. On a visit to Rome he was appalled by the corruption and immorality he saw in the clergy from the papacy down. His last lingering doubt regarding conditions seems to have been removed while penitently ascending on his knees the sacred stairs of the Lateran, when he seemed to hear an inner voice declaring, "The just shall live by faith."

146

SCENE 16

[LUTHER *is nailing his theses to the church door, with several friends* (CITIZENS) *standing near by.*]

RELIGION [*during tableau*]—Arriving home, he drew up ninety-five theses, or statements, opposing conditions, which he posted on the door of the Wittenberg Church. This was the beginning of his public conflict with Rome and was "the spark that set Europe aflame." Three years later he was excommunicated by the pope, but he publicly burned the bull of excommunication together with copies of laws made by the Roman Church. A year later he was summoned to the Diet of Worms and there ordered to retract. He replied that he could retract nothing, except what was disproved by Scripture or reason, exclaiming, "Here I stand; I can do naught else; so help me, God!" En route home he was seized by friends and hid for about a year, during which time he translated the New Testament into the German language. Later he returned to Wittenberg, dwelling calmly for twenty-four years in full publicity, preaching and teaching, writing books and pamphlets of all sorts to explain and uphold his doctrines, living in perfect safety and dying in tranquility, honored and beloved by his countrymen and by thousands in other lands. He was no longer a voice in the wilderness; he was the leader of a mighty movement, the hero of the Protestant cause.

CURTAIN

CHOIR—"A Mighty Fortress Is Our God." [*Two verses.*]

HISTORY—Among the faculty and students of Wittenberg who stood faithfully behind Luther was a young man named Philip Melancthon. He had taken his master's degree at seventeen and was made full professor at twenty-one. He became not only Luther's closest friend, but the foremost scholar of the Reformation. Before Luther posted his theses there appeared in the University of Paris and elsewhere in France men who, from their study of the Scriptures, had come to entertain opinions very similar to those of the German reformer, and the land again soon became filled with so-called heretics, who became known as Huguenots, and numbered about 400,000, including many of the nobility and higher classes.

SCENE 17

[*Street scene in Paris, where company of men* (EXECUTIONERS) *with clubs and daggers are in position of murdering a group of people* (CITIZENS OF PARIS).]

RELIGION [*during tableau*]—Several massacres followed, the one on Saint Bartholomew's Day in Paris being one of the worst crimes in history, the victims numbering between 20,000 and 30,000. However, instead of exterminating the Huguenots, the massacre only served to arouse them to a more determined defense of their faith, and finally, under Henry IV, they were granted freedom of worship and several fortified towns as places of refuge.

CURTAIN

CHOIR—"Lead On, O King Eternal." [*Two verses.*]

HISTORY—The Reformation in the Netherlands fills a heroic page of Protestant history. A Dutch translation of the Bible was published, and within a few years twenty-five editions appeared. The Inquisition was established in full force, and the first Protestant martyrs, Henry Voes and John Esch, were burned at the stake. The real crisis, however, did not arrive until Philip II came to the throne of Spain and endeavored to wipe out Protestantism from this part of his domain. From his Dutch subjects came the prompt reply, "We are ready to die for the gospel."

SCENE 18

[*Street where a* GROUP OF HOLLANDERS *are listening to a* PREACHER.]

RELIGION [*during tableau*]—At first they held their meetings at night in woods and desolate places; but soon, growing bolder, they marched through the streets of the towns, singing psalms, and armed themselves to defend their preachers, while speaking. When some extremists indulged in imagebreaking, the terrible Duke of Alva was sent with 10,000 troops to subdue the Netherlands. In the reign of terror that followed, executions by the wholesale are recorded, 1,500 being taken in their beds on Ash Wednesday morning, and later 800 more, all of whom Alva ordered to be executed.

CURTAIN

HISTORY—The only hope of the Netherlands was in the noble Prince of Orange, William the Silent. Defeated by land, he armed the Dutch sailors, who scattered the Spanish fleet, took its admiral prisoner and forced Alva to leave the country. Still the war continued, reaching its climax in the heroic defense of Leyden. The dykes were cut and the sea let in, thus admitting the Dutch sailors with supplies. The Spaniards fled, and within a short time the northern provinces of the Netherlands renounced allegiance to the king of Spain and declared themselves an independent republic. Thirty years of struggle followed, during which William of Orange fell at the hand of Philip's hired assassin, but nothing could stamp out the spirit of freedom or the undying faith of the little republic.

CHOIR—"I Will Sing the Wondrous Story." [*One verse.*]

HISTORY—The great challenge to the papacy from Switzerland was launched by Ulrich Zwingli, who was appalled and disgusted with religious conditions and made severe attacks upon the abuses of the church. He preached in Zurich, and within five years had removed all evidence of Romish pomp and ceremony and had supervised a Swiss version of the Bible.

SCENE 19

[*A battlefield, with* ZWINGLI *wounded and supported by several* SWISS SOLDIERS.]

RELIGION [*during tableau*]—Seven years later, when hostilities broke out between the Catholic and Protestant states, Zwingli, armed and mounted, rode with his people into battle. He made no use of his weapons, but cheered on the soldiers and assured them that God would prosper the good cause. Soon after the battle began he was wounded and fell, declaring, "They may kill the body, but they can not kill the soul." Some of the enemy tried to make him confess to a priest, or invoke the saints, but he shook his head; and one of them finally thrust him through with a sword, exclaiming, "Die, obstinate heretic!" They burned his body and scattered the ashes.

CURTAIN

CHOIR—"Beneath the Cross of Jesus." [*Two verses.*]

SCENE 20

[CALVIN *preaching to* CITIZENS OF GENEVA.]

RELIGION [*during tableau*]—John Calvin was born and educated in France. When he embraced the Reformed teachings he was forced to flee, and made Geneva, French Switzerland, his home. His academy became one of the chief centers of Protestantism in Europe, and he is regarded as one of the greatest thinkers of Christendom since Augustine. Strongly opposed to organic union of church and state, his teachings have been a mighty influence for democracy throughout the world. He preached for twenty-three years in Geneva, which became a model community under his leadership. He died at the age of fifty-four, and by his own request was buried in an unmarked grave, so that, like Moses, "no man knoweth his sepulchre."

CURTAIN

CHOIR—"Saviour, More than Life." [*Two verses.*]

SCENE 21

[LEFEVRE *handing books to a group of* CITIZENS OF PARIS.]

RELIGION [*during tableau*]—The persecution which had driven Calvin from France began when Jacques Lefevre, "the real beginner of the Reformation in France," had published a revised edition of an old French translation of the Bible, believing that the Scriptures should be in the hands of the people. The Parliament took stern measures to suppress all books embodying Reformed doctrines, publicly burned Lefevre's translation, and compelled the author and his friends to take refuge in Strasburg. Afterwards they were restored to royal favor, but later, during the persecution of the Huguenots, or French Protestants, they were burned.

CURTAIN

CHOIR—"Tell Me the Old, Old Story." [*One verse.*]

SCENE 22

[TYNDALE *is seated at a table, which is covered with manuscripts.*]

RELIGION [*during tableau*]—William Tyndale, a leader of the Reformation in England, is known as the "Father of the Open Bible." He was a student at both Oxford and

Cambridge, during which time he was inspired to make a translation of the New Testament into English so that the common people might read it. Banished from London, he took refuge in Germany, but was bitterly persecuted there also, until a copy of the complete New Testament was finally sent to England, where it was violently attacked by the bishops. Any one found with a copy was forced to burn it, but within a few years 15,000 copies had been circulated. Tyndale's Bible, perhaps the greatest achievement in English history, was revised by Coverdale and issued as Cromwell's Bible, and later, as Cranmer's Bible, was set up in every church in England. This same Bible was brought by the Puritan Fathers to the New World and fixed the standard of English in America. No book ever published has had so great and lasting an influence on the purity of language and the style of prose. Tyndale was captured by treachery and suffered a martyr's death at Antwerp, praying with his last breath, "Lord, open the king of England's eyes!"

CHOIR—"How Precious Is the Book Divine." [*Two verses.*]

HISTORY—Tyndale's prayer was right speedily answered, though by strange means. The man who was most instrumental in making the Bible free to the people of England was Thomas Cranmer, Archbishop of Canterbury. In helping Henry VIII secure divorce from his queen, Catherine of Aragon, he brought about a complete rupture between England and Rome, and opened the door to the Reformation. Cranmer immediately recommended for official adoption a translation of the Scriptures, which, under another name, was practically that of Tyndale. There were prompt Romanist reactions, charges of heresy against Cranmer and denunciations against the new translation. Henry became more capricious and brutal every day, persecuting Protestants and

Catholics impartially. On one day three Lutheran clergymen were burned for heresy and three Romanists tortured and beheaded for denying the king's supremacy. Cranmer came safely through it all, though threatened as often as the more outspoken preachers, Ridley and Latimer. He was a constructive rather than a destructive reformer, and all through the brief reign of the boy king Edward he went quietly on building up the English Church. Too soon the gentler days of Edward were over and the Romanist princess, Mary Tudor, ascended the throne. Then hundreds of Protestant martyrs passed through the flames, including the loyal Latimer and Ridley, the former exhorting his companion, "Play the man, Master Ridley, for by God's grace we shall this day light such a candle in England as will never be put out."

SCENE 23

[*A courtyard, where* CRANMER *is tied to a stake, surrounded by brush, under which is a powerful red light.* EXECUTIONERS *and witnesses* (CITIZENS OF ENGLAND) *stand near by.*]

RELIGION [*during tableau*]—Finally Cranmer was condemned as a traitor, cast into prison and told he must die. Then his courage gave way; he consented to sign a sweeping recantation, condemning all Protestant teachings as heresy. It failed to save him. But when he stood in view of the stake courage returned. He repudiated all his recantations, declared the pope to be Antichrist, and steadfastly held in the flame his right hand, which had signed the denial, saying with a loud voice, "This hand hath offended!" Without a cry or a groan he passed manfully to stand before the tribunal of God.

CURTAIN

CHOIR—"O Jesus, I Have Promised." [*One verse.*]

HISTORY—Meanwhile in Scotland a man of different type had arisen—John Knox, the "Scottish Elijah." Of all the Reformers, his life is one of the most dramatic. Quietly preaching in the town of St. Andrews, at the age of thirty-two, he was interrupted by the arrival of a French fleet, which battered the walls of the castle until it was obliged to surrender, carried off all the inmates to France and made them galley slaves. After nineteen months of torture the English Government procured their release and Knox spent nearly five years preaching in England; but when Queen Mary came to the throne he dared to rebuke the multitude for rejoicing, then crossed the Channel and joined Calvin in Geneva.

SCENE 24

[KNOX *is preaching to a* GROUP OF SCOTCHMEN.]

RELIGION [*during tableau*]—Knox later revisited Scotland to find the Reformation in full swing, and preached boldly in Edinburgh, then returned to Geneva. A year later, when many of the Scottish nobles and gentry signed the first "Covenant" organizing themselves as Protestants, Knox, by his writings, upheld and greatly strengthened the movement; and when Queen Mary's death brought her Protestant sister, Elizabeth, to the throne, he finally returned to Scotland, to help in establishing the Reformed Church on a strong basis.

CURTAIN

CHOIR—"Faith Is the Victory." [*One verse.*]

HISTORY—John Wesley was brought up in the country parsonage of Epworth, his forefathers for three generations being clergymen of the Church of England. John and his brother Charles, five years younger, were students in Christ Church College, Oxford, when the famous "Holy Club" was organized for study and prayer. They condemned the formalism and worldliness which were devitalizing the church. Their methodical lives led to their being dubbed "Methodists." After becoming ministers of the Anglican Church, the Wesley brothers spent ten years as missionaries in Georgia. Returning to London, they pressed their Reformation with vigor.

SCENE 25

[WESLEY *is preaching in a chapel, and both he and members of the congregation* (CITIZENS OF ENGLAND) *are in position of shielding themselves from "stones" and "clubs" in the hands of a small mob* (CITIZENS OF ENGLAND).]

RELIGION [*during tableau*]—It would take too long to tell of the persecutions which the early followers of Wesley endured. Stone-throwing and window-smashing were the least of the violent acts of the mobs aroused by their fearless preaching. But so persistent and courageous were they that public sentiment began to change and their journeys became like a royal progress. John Wesley continued preaching until his eighty-eighth year, and became one of the best beloved men in the kingdom. His brother Charles was author of nearly seven thousand hymns.

CURTAIN

CHOIR—"Faith Is the Victory." [*Second verse.*]

HISTORY—Tertullian wrote, "The blood of the martyrs was the seed of the church." By men and women in thousands who have followed, and who would not deny their faith in Jesus, the gospel of Christ has been handed down to us through the centuries. If every one today who professes to be a follower of the Saviour would be as loyal as our fathers, the world could be won in this generation.

CHOIR—"Faith of Our Fathers" [*while audience leaves*].

The Pharisee from Tarsus

Tableau with Song and Story

SCENES FROM THE MINISTRY OF PAUL, THE GREAT MISSIONARY

CHARACTERS

READER.

PAUL_____The Pharisee from Tarsus

BARNABAS, SILAS, TIMOTHY, LUKE

                    His Traveling Companions

STEPHEN_____A Loyal Christian

JUDAS_____A Citizen of Damascus

ANANIAS_____A Devout Jew of Damascus

ELYMAS _____A Sorcerer

SERGIUS PAULUS_____Governor of Cyprus

JASON_____A Man of Macedonia

LYDIA_____A Merchant of Philippi

THREE WOMEN_____Her Servants

ADINA_____An Insane Fortune Teller

HORUS_____Her Master

LYSIAS_____Captain of the Guard

SEVEN EXORCISTS_____Sons of Sceva

FELIX CLAUDIUS_____Governor of Judea

PORCIUS FESTUS_____Governor of Judea

HEROD AGRIPPA_____The King

TERTULLUS_____A Lawyer from Jerusalem

ANANIAS_____The High Priest

PARMA_____Captain of a Ship

JULIUS_____Captain of Imperial Regiment

PUBLIUS_____Governor of Malta

157

Two Temple Officers.

Angel.

Citizens of Antioch, Lystra, Philippi, Athens, Jerusalem
and Cæsarea.

Natives of Malta.

Sailors and Prisoners on the Ship.

Soldiers.

The Jailer.

COSTUMES

Paul.

Flowing robe of white, made from a sheet or a flannel night dress.
He has two shoulder scarfs or cloaks, one red and one blue or
with stripes, which he alternates in various scenes. In the first
sixteen scenes he has dark hair and beard. In remaining scenes he
wears a white wig and beard. Perhaps two men could take the
part.

Barnabas, Silas, Luke.

Costumes similar to Paul's, but of different colors. Dark beards.
Turbans made from a large square of cloth bound with a colored
band.

Timothy.

A younger man, without beard. Costumes similar to others.

Stephen.

Costumes similar to others. Gray beard.

Judas and Ananias.

Use Silas and Luke.

Elymas.

A short man with dark beard. Costume like others.

Sergius Paulus

Robe of bright color with cape of contrasting color; dark beard
and turban of bright cloth.

Jason.

Use Luke.

Lydia and All Other Women.

Flowing gowns of bright colors, with scarfs over heads, falling on
back of neck. Adina, the fortune teller, should have a bright

red dress, with beads and bracelets, the latter also being worn by other women, except servants.

HORUS.

Rough-looking man with dark beard. Has a whip.

LYSIAS AND OTHER GUARDS.

Knee-length tunic of red, with yellow girdle. The tunic may be edged with a Roman design in purple and gold. Helmet made from a folded piece of gilt paper. Large circular shield and spear. Brown socks, with sandals laced high. No beard.

SEVEN SONS OF SCEVA.

Use men representing BARNABAS, SILAS, LUKE, TIMOTHY, STEPHEN, ELYMAS and HORUS, all with bright scarfs draped around waist instead of over the shoulder.

FELIX AND FESTUS.

Flowing robes of rich colors, with cape of contrasting colors. One wears a short, dark beard and the other a longer beard. Low crown of gold.

AGRIPPA.

Use man representing SERGIUS PAULUS, with a crown of gold instead of turban. No beard.

TERTULLUS.

Use man representing BARNABAS, with turban of white.

ANANIAS, THE HIGH PRIEST.

Robe of white, reaching to ankles. Over this a cloak of soft blue material (outing), with elbow-length sleeves and knee-length coat. Over this a short skirt of deep lace. Square, white "bib" with twelve criss-crosses of colored crayons. White turban coiled high, and with square of gold paper in front.

PARMA.

Robe of white, reaching halfway between knees and ankles, and girded at the waist. Turban of white. Short, gray beard. The man representing STEPHEN may be used for this character also.

JULIUS.

Use man representing LYSIAS.

PUBLIUS.

Use the man representing FELIX, with slight change.

ANGEL.

> Use one of the men wearing a sheet drapery, with long folds draped over arms, which are raised for "wings."

CITIZENS.

> Men and women with flowing robes of all colors, prepared as described above. Children are similarly dressed.

SAILORS.

> Use a few of the men who were citizens, with bright cloaks removed, appearing only in tunics.

PRISONERS.

> Same arrangement as for SAILORS.

ALL MEN.

> Bare legs and bedroom slippers or sandals.

PREPARATION

Same as for pageant "Soldiers of the Cross."

SONGS AND STORIES

PRELIMINARY

READER—Acts 6: 7-15; 7: 1-4, 51-60.

SCENE 1

PAUL THE PERSECUTOR

READER—Acts 8: 1b-4.
CHOIR—"Faith of Our Fathers."

SCENE 2

THE CALLING OF PAUL

READER—Acts 9: 1-7.
　　　　　Acts 9: 8-16 (explanatory).
CHOIR—"Holy Ghost, with Light Divine."

SCENE 3

SAUL'S CONVERSION

READER—Acts 9: 17, 18.

    Acts 9: 19-22 (explanatory).

    Acts 9: 23-30; 11: 19-25.

CHOIR—"Open My Eyes."

SCENE 4

WITH BARNABAS IN ANTIOCH

READER—Acts 11: 26; 13: 1-3.

    Acts 13: 4, 5 (explanatory).

CHOIR—"Come, Thou Fount of Every Blessing."

SCENE 5

A SORCERER REBUKED

READER—Acts 13: 6-12.

    Acts 14: 1-10 (explanatory).

CHOIR—"Ye Servants of God."

SCENE 6

CROWNED AS A GOD

READER—Acts 14: 11-18.

    Acts 14: 19-28; 15: 1, 2, 4, 22, 30, 36-41;

    16: 1-5 (explanatory).

CHOIR—"Ye Christian Heralds, Go Proclaim."

SCENE 7

THE VISION AT TROAS

READER—Acts 16: 6-10.

    Acts 16: 11, 12 (explanatory).

CHOIR—"We've a Story to Tell to the Nations."

SCENE 8

THE CONVERSION OF LYDIA

READER—Acts 16: 13-15.
CHOIR—"O Zion, Haste!"

SCENE 9

A DEMON CAST OUT

READER—Acts 16: 16-18.
          Acts 16: 19-24 (explanatory).
CHOIR—"Just as I Am."

SCENE 10

DELIVERED FROM PRISON

READER—Acts 16: 25-28.
          Acts 16: 29-40; 17: 15-21 (explanatory).
CHOIR—"He Leadeth Me."

SCENE 11

THE UNKNOWN GOD

READER—Acts 17: 22-33.
          Acts 18: 1-11, 18-20; 19: 1b-12 (explanatory).
CHOIR—"Hail to the Brightness."

SCENE 12

EXORCISTS REBUKED

READER—Acts 19: 13-20.
          Acts 19: 21, 22 (explanatory).
CHOIR—"Come, Ye Disconsolate."

SCENE 13

Farewell to Asia

Reader—Acts 20: 17-38.
Choir—"God Be with You."

SCENE 14

Arrested in Jerusalem

Reader—Acts 21: 17, 26-30.
Choir—"Who Is on the Lord's Side?"

SCENE 15

Rescued by the Guards

Reader—Acts 21: 31-39a; 22: 22-24.
       Acts 22: 25-30 (explanatory).
Choir—"Stand Up for Jesus."

SCENE 16

Before the Council

Reader—Acts 23: 1-9.
       Acts 23: 10-16, 22-35 (explanatory).
Choir—"In the Hour of Trial."

SCENE 17

Before Felix

Reader—Acts 24: 1, 9-22.
       Acts 24: 23-37; 25: 1-6 (explanatory).
Choir—"Jesus Calls Us."

SCENE 18

Before Festus

Reader—Acts 25: 7-12.
        Acts 25: 13-22 (explanatory).
Choir—"O Could I Speak the Matchless Worth."

SCENE 19

Before Agrippa

Reader—Acts 25: 23-27; 26: 1-7, 21-29.
        Acts 26: 30-32; 27: 1-20 (explanatory).
Choir—"My Jesus, as Thou Wilt."

SCENE 20

En Route to Rome

Reader—Acts 27: 21-26.
        Acts 27: 36-44 (explanatory).
Choir—"From Every Stormy Wind that Blows."

SCENE 21

Shipwrecked at Melita

Reader—Acts 28: 1-6.
        Acts 28: 7-15 (explanatory).
Choir—"Jesus, Saviour, Pilot Me."

SCENE 22

Located in Rome

Reader—Acts 28: 16, 23-31.
Choir—"O Jesus, I Have Promised."

TABLEAUX

SCENE 1

A Room in Jerusalem: SAUL, with a whip, is threatening a group kneeling in prayer. SOLDIERS stand in background.

SCENE 2

A Road: SAUL is lying upon the ground with ANGEL standing near, arms outstretched. Spotlight on them. Two men standing near by.

SCENE 3

A Room in Damascus: ANANIAS, the Jew, stands in center of room, his hands upon the head of SAUL, who kneels before him. JUDAS stands at one side of room and two men at the other side.

SCENE 4

A Room in Antioch: SAUL is standing, as if preaching to a group of people, the latter being seated informally in a group. SAUL'S arms are slightly extended. BARNABAS stands near him.

SCENE 5

A Room in the Palace at Paphos: SERGIUS is seated in an elevated chair, leaning forward in attitude of wonder. PAUL stands before him at a distance. ELYMAS is at one side, upon his knees, with right arm raised over his eyes. PAUL is pointing directly at ELYMAS.

SCENE 6

A Street in Lystra: Stalls or booths at rear, where merchandise is displayed. PAUL and BARNABAS stand in center, with LYSTRIANS arranging garlands of flowers upon them.

SCENE 7

Room in a House in Troas: PAUL lies on a cot at one side, raising himself slightly upon one arm to get vision of JASON (man of Macedonia), who stands near by. Spotlight upon the latter.

SCENE 8

Outside the Wall of Philippi: LYDIA, her THREE SERVANTS and a group of women are seated on the ground, looking at PAUL, BARNABAS, SILAS and TIMOTHY, who stand at a distance.

SCENE 9

A Street in Philippi: ADINA sits cross-legged at back center, with HORUS standing near her. Group of people at left. PAUL, SILAS, BARNABAS and TIMOTHY at right. PAUL'S hands are extended toward ADINA.

SCENE 10

In a Prison at Philippi: Several stools, a pile of blankets and several water jars. PAUL and SILAS stand near right center, with the JAILER upon his knees before them. A GUARD stands at door. Other PRISONERS in a group behind PAUL and SILAS.

SCENE 11

On Mars Hill at Athens: Outdoor scene. PAUL is standing upon an elevation in rear center, with a group of citizens assembled before him.

SCENE 12

A Room in Ephesus: The SEVEN SONS OF SCEVA are trying to hold a demoniac, who is straining every muscle to get away from them.

SCENE 13

A Room in Miletus: PAUL stands in center of a group of men and women who kneel around him, weeping.

SCENE 14

In the Temple at Jerusalem: Two pillars are placed right and left to represent the temple. Mob surrounds PAUL, one member grasping him roughly.

SCENE 15

On the Temple Steps: PAUL stands on center of top step, with Roman guards on each side of him. Space below is swarming with a mob.

SCENE 16

The Council Room in Jerusalem: PAUL stands bound between two guards in front of the HIGH PRIEST, who sits upon an elevated dais. Members of the Sanhedrin are seated at right and left of platform.

SCENE 17

The Council Room in Cæsarea: Arrangement similar to Scene 16. FELIX is seated upon the dais, with PAUL and guards in front of him. TERTULLUS stands near. Group of Jews seated at right and left.

SCENE 18

The Council Room in Cæsarea: Same arrangement as in Scene 17, with FESTUS and ANANIAS seated upon the dais.

SCENE 19

The Council Room in Cæsarea: Same arrangement as in Scene 18. FESTUS and AGRIPPA are seated upon the dais, with heads close together, as if in consultation.

SCENE 20

On a Ship: Boxes covered with tarpaulin at left and bags of grain at right. PAUL stands in center, with arms extended. PARMA, JULIUS, SAILORS and PRISONERS are grouped upon their knees around him.

SCENE 21

On the Island Melita: All characters of Scene 20 are grouped around a fire in center of stage. PAUL stands near fire, with arm extended and a snake hanging from it. PUBLIUS and natives stand at sides, watching.

SCENE 22

A Room in Rome: PAUL is seated in center, with a group of people seated around him, leaning forward in attitude of attention. JULIUS stands at rear center.

Soldiers of the Cross

Tableau with Song and Story

SCENES FROM THE MINISTRY OF THE TWELVE APOSTLES

CHARACTERS

READER.

TWELVE APOSTLES (Matthias in place of Judas).

SPECTATORS (men, women and children).

PRIESTS AND SCRIBES.

TWO SOLDIERS (more, if desired).

ANGEL.

SEVEN DEACONS.

STEPHEN.

SIMON, THE SORCERER.

PRISONERS.

ÆNEAS.

DORCAS.

CORNELIUS.

LAME MAN.

PAUL.

PHILIP.

COSTUMES

APOSTLES.

Tunics of various colors, with large shoulder scarfs of contrasting colors. Striped outing-flannel nightgowns make excellent tunics and should reach just below the knees. Head scarfs tied with ribbons.

WOMEN.

Flowing dresses of bright colors, reaching to ankles, with head scarfs and girdles of contrasting colors. Beads, earrings and bracelets.

169

CHILDREN.

> The girls are dressed similar to the women. Boys wear tunics like the men, but no turbans.

PRIESTS AND SCRIBES.

> Tunics should reach to the ankles, and turbans should be of white, coiled high (bath towels are excellent). Women's smocks of plain colors or stripes (no flowers) may be worn as "coats," in place of shoulder scarfs, as the apostles wear.

SIMON, STEPHEN, ÆNEAS AND THE DEACONS.

> Similar to APOSTLES.

CORNELIUS.

> Knee-length tunic, with bright girdle and cape of contrasting colors hanging from back of shoulders, reaching to knees. Brown socks with sandals laced high over them. Helmet with fan-shaped ornament in front. A sheet of gold-colored paper fitted tightly to the head makes an excellent helmet.

SOLDIERS.

> Similar to CORNELIUS, without the cape.

ANGEL.

> Usual robe of white, with wings.

PREPARATION

The tableaux are to be presented as "painted pictures"—all characters standing perfectly still while the story is read, and the scenes being changed while hymns are sung.

Very little scenery is needed, simple draperies being used for backgrounds. If not available, use folding screens. The temple steps should be about twelve feet long and constructed of lumber, the upper platform being about three feet deep. Movable pillars one foot square may be made of wallboard.

If the front of the stage is hung with a tarlatan curtain, the scenes will appear as deep, beautiful pictures.

Every character in the pageant should have a typed list of the scenes, checking those in which he appears, so they may take their positions quickly. A stage assistant should have large cards announcing the scenes to follow.

SONGS AND STORIES

PRELIMINARY

CHRIST'S LAST COMMAND

CHOIR—"Follow the Gleam."
READER—Acts 1: 1-14.

SCENE 1

DESCENT OF THE HOLY GHOST

CHOIR—"Holy Ghost, with Light Divine."
READER—Acts 2: 1-4.

SCENE 2

PETER'S SERMON

CHOIR—"Ye Servants of God."
READER—Acts 2: 5-47.

SCENE 3

A LAME MAN HEALED

CHOIR—"Jesus Saves."
READER—Acts 3: 1-10.

SCENE 4

PETER'S SERMON

CHOIR—"O Zion, Haste."
READER—Acts 3: 11-19.

SCENE 5

PETER AND JOHN ARRESTED

CHOIR—"Stand Up for Jesus."
READER—Acts 4: 1-4.

SCENE 6

SESSION OF THE COUNCIL

CHOIR—"Jesus Calls Us."
READER—Acts 4: 5-23.

SCENE 7

MINISTRY OF THE APOSTLES

CHOIR—"Lead On, O King Eternal."
READER—Acts 5: 12-16.

SCENE 8

IMPRISONED AND RELEASED

CHOIR—"God Will Take Care of You."
READER—Acts 5: 17-20.
       Acts 5: 21-26 (explanatory).

SCENE 9

TRIED AND DISMISSED

CHOIR—"All the Way My Saviour Leads Me."
READER—Acts 5: 27-39.
       Acts 5: 40-42; 6: 1-4 (explanatory).

SCENE 10

DEACONS ORDAINED

CHOIR—"Stepping in the Light."
READER—Acts 6: 5-8.

SCENE 11

STEPHEN BEFORE THE COUNCIL

CHOIR—"In the Hour of Trial."
READER—Acts 6: 9-15; 7: 1-4, 51-56.

SCENE 12

STEPHEN IS STONED

CHOIR—"Faith of Our Fathers."
READER—Acts 7: 57-60.
(The following scenes are optional.)

SCENE 13

PHILIP PREACHES IN SAMARIA

CHOIR—"Ye Christian Heralds, Go, Proclaim."
READER—Acts 8: 5-13.

SCENE 14

PETER HEALS ÆNEAS

CHOIR—"Rescue the Perishing."
READER—Acts 9: 32-35.

SCENE 15

PETER HEALS DORCAS

CHOIR—"The Great Physician."
READER—Acts 9: 36-41.
　　　　　Acts 10: 1-8, 21-26 (explanatory).

SCENE 16

CONVERSION OF CORNELIUS

CHOIR—"We've a Story to Tell to the Nations."
READER—Acts 10: 27, 28, 34-45.

TABLEAUX

SCENE 1

A Room in Jerusalem: The TWELVE APOSTLES are kneeling, with ANGEL on an elevation in rear center.

SCENE 2

A Street, with Steps of Temple in Rear: PETER stands on steps with APOSTLES on each side. Groups of men, women and children (SPECTATORS) listening, in attitudes of amazement.

SCENE 3

Same as Scene 2: PETER and JOHN on steps. PETER leaning forward and grasping hand of LAME MAN, who has crutch. SPECTATORS amazed.

SCENE 4

Solomon's Porch: Several tall pillars on platform. PETER in center, surrounded by group of SPECTATORS.

SCENE 5

Same as Scene 4: SOLDIERS holding PETER and JOHN, with PRIESTS near by and SPECTATORS backing away.

SCENE 6

The Council Room: Steps of the temple may be used to represent a throne, on which the HIGH PRIEST is seated in a large chair, surrounded by other PRIESTS. PETER and JOHN standing in front of them, with guards (SOLDIERS).

SCENE 7

Same as Scene 4: PETER and JOHN healing afflicted, surrounded by multitude of SPECTATORS.

SCENE 8

Room in a Prison: Several stools and a pile of blankets and several water jars. Dim light. ANGEL at right, with arm extended toward door. PETER and JOHN in center, facing door. Other PRISONERS sleeping.

SCENE 9

Council Room as in Scene 6: Gamaliel (the PRIEST) stands amongst other PRIESTS, with one hand extended toward PRISONERS and one toward the HIGH PRIEST.

SCENE 10

A Room: The SEVEN DEACONS are kneeling in front of the TWELVE APOSTLES, the latter standing with arms raised in benediction.

SCENE 11

The Council Room, as in Scene 9: STEPHEN, between two guards (SOLDIERS), stands with hands clasped and face uplifted.

SCENE 12

Outside the City Gate: STEPHEN is lying upon the ground, one arm upraised, to ward off stones being hurled at him by angry Jews (men SPECTATORS). The HIGH PRIEST stands at one side and SAUL at the other, the latter holding STEPHEN's outer cloak. Inflated bags will serve as stones, many being scattered about.

SCENE 13

A Street in Samaria: PHILIP in rear center, with SIMON THE SORCERER kneeling in front of him, surrounded by a multitude (SPECTATORS).

SCENE 14

A Room in Lydda: ÆNEAS sitting on a bed or couch, with PETER holding his hand. Several people watching in amazement.

SCENE 15

Room Similar to Scene 14: DORCAS stands beside the bed, with PETER holding one of her hands as if presenting her to group of women (SPECTATORS) who stand at one side.

SCENE 16

Room in Cæsarea: PETER stands in center, preaching, with CORNELIUS in front. Others (SPECTATORS) sitting and standing.

The Story that Never Grows Old

A PAGEANT FOR CHRISTMAS

CHARACTERS

READER.	THREE SHEPHERDS.
ADULT CHOIR.	THREE WISE-MEN, OR KINGS.
CHILDREN'S CHORUS.	HEROD.
ANGEL.	ROYAL ATTENDANTS.
MARY.	REPRESENTATIVES OF NATIONS.
JOSEPH.	CANDLE BEARERS.

COSTUMES

READER.

May wear modern dress or a flowing robe. Has scroll with manuscript attached.

ADULT CHOIR.

May wear modern dress or surplice.

CHILDREN'S CHORUS.

This group includes REPRESENTATIVES OF NATIONS and is in rear of auditorium while it sings.

ANGEL.

Flowing robe of white, with wings.

MARY.

Girl of about seventeen years. Robe of gray, with dark-blue girdle and white scarf over head.

JOSEPH.

Man of middle age, with dark hair and beard. Robe of dark blue, yellow girdle, shoulder scarf of red or striped cloth, and small turban of yellow. Carries staff.

177

SHEPHERDS.

Tunics of dark material, reaching just below knees; capes of dark brown, green and purple. Small turbans. One has a flute, one a gourd and one a crook.

WISE-MEN, OR KINGS.

According to tradition, one was an Egyptian, one a Hindu and one a Greek.

The Egyptian should be a man of dark skin, with dark beard. Wears a white robe reaching to ankles and open at throat. Sash of bright blue. Cloak of brown, edged with yellow; it reaches to ankles and has sleeves of elbow length, permitting sleeves of shirt to show. Turban of red silk.

The Hindu also is of dark skin, with white hair and beard. White shirt and white wide-flowing breeches, gathered at the ankle. White cloak. Turban made of white shawl. Red slippers.

The Greek is of smaller build, but heavy. Fair complexion; light hair, without a covering. White tunic made knee length, with short sleeves and gathered at the waist with a band. (A white night dress will serve.) Bare legs and sandals on feet. Bright scarf around shoulders.

HEROD.

Man with white beard. Robe of purple, bordered with red and a girdle of gold. Cap of crimson which falls down over back of neck and shoulders. Narrow crown of gold paper holds the cap in place.

ROYAL ATTENDANTS.

Two boys or young men wearing knee-length tunics (night dresses), with girdles and capes of bright cloth. Bare legs and sandals. Heads bare.

REPRESENTATIVES OF NATIONS.

See section on "Costumes." Each country may have as many representatives as desired, but two for each will be sufficient.

CANDLE BEARERS.

These may wear modern dress or flowing robes or surplices of black and white.

ARRANGEMENT

The stage is arranged with upper and lower platforms, the former being the larger. The king's throne is arranged on the lower, and the manger, with a low stool beside it, is on the upper. Tall white candles are burning at extreme right and left of the altar, with others ready to be lighted in the windows and other stations.

PAGEANT

CHOIR—"O Little Town of Bethlehem" [*four verses*]. [*Stage empty. Dim, blue light.*]

READER—"And in the sixth month the angel Gabriel was sent from God unto a city of Galilee, named Nazareth, to a virgin espoused to a man whose name was Joseph, of the house of David; and the virgin's name was Mary. And the angel came in unto her and said:

[ANGEL *enters on lower platform from left with lily in hand.* MARY *enters from right and kneels, facing* ANGEL, *body upright, head bowed and hands clasped.*]

ORGAN—"Ave Maria" [*played softly during the annunciation*].

ANGEL—"Hail, thou that art highly favored, the Lord is with thee; blessed art thou among women. Fear not, Mary, for thou hast found favor with God. And behold, thou shalt bring forth a son called the Son of the Highest, and the Lord God shall give him the throne of his father David. And he shall reign over the house of Jacob for ever; and of his kingdom there shall be no end. The Holy Ghost shall come upon thee; therefore, also, that holy thing which shall be born of thee shall be called the Son of God."

CHOIR OR SOLO BY MARY—"Magnificat." [*During the singing the* ANGEL *turns slowly and mounts to the higher platform.* MARY *lifts her head to the* CHOIR, *but remains*

179

kneeling, in adoration. She exits right, during the following reading.]

READER—"And it came to pass in those days that there went out a decree from Cæsar Augustus, that all the world should be taxed, and every one went into his own city. And Joseph also went up from Galilee, out of the city of Nazareth, because he was of the house and lineage of David, to be taxed with Mary his espoused wife, being great with child. And so it was that, while they were there, the days were accomplished that she should be delivered. And she brought forth her first-born son, and wrapped him in swaddling clothes, and laid him in a manger, because there was no room for them in the inn."

CHOIR—"Once in David's Royal City" [*vs. 1, 2 and 6*]. [MARY *and* JOSEPH *enter right, go to the upper platform and form a tableau around the manger,* MARY *sitting on a stool and* JOSEPH *standing, leaning upon his staff. As* MARY *seats herself she turns on a light bulb concealed in straw in manger.*]

CHILDREN'S CHORUS—"Away in a Manger [*vs. 1 and 2, sung softly in the distance*].

CHOIR—"Noel" [*vs. 1 and 2*].

ORGAN—Piping music, imitating shepherd's pipe. [*The* THREE SHEPHERDS *enter, one with pipe, one with gourd and one with crook.* SHEPHERD *pretends to pipe while music lasts. They stand at right while* ANGEL *and* READER *speak.*]

READER—"And there were shepherds in the same country abiding in the fields, keeping watch over their flocks by night. And lo, the angel of the Lord came upon them, and the glory of the Lord shone round about them, and they were sore afraid. [*Spotlight on* ANGEL.] And the angel said unto them,

ANGEL—"Fear not; for behold, I bring you good tidings of great joy, which shall be to all people. For unto you is born this day in the city of David a Saviour, which is Christ the Lord. And this shall be a sign unto you: Ye shall find the babe wrapped in swaddling clothes, lying in a manger.

READER—"And suddenly there was with the angel a multitude of the heavenly host, praising God, and saying, Glory to God in the highest, and on earth, peace and good will to men. [*If desired, the* CHOIR *may sing the anthem* "Glory to God in the Highest."]

CHILDREN'S CHORUS—"It Came Upon the Midnight Clear" [*one verse*].

CHOIR—"Alleluia" chant.

ONE SHEPHERD—"Let us now go even unto Bethlehem and see this thing which is come to pass, which the Lord hath made known unto us."

ANOTHER SHEPHERD—"Verily, let us go at once."

[SHEPHERDS *go to upper platform, two kneeling and one standing beside the manger, while* CHOIR *sings.*]

CHOIR—"Hark! the Herald Angels Sing" [*one verse*].

SOLO—"Lullaby" [*by soprano soloist or by* MARY *herself*].

CHOIR—"Noel" [*vs. 3, 4 and 5*]. [SHEPHERDS *retire to side of platform.*]

ORGAN—"Marche Royale" [*while* HEROD *ascends to throne with attendants*].

READER—"Now when Jesus was born in Bethlehem of Judæa in the days of Herod the king, behold, there came wise men from the east to Jerusalem, saying, Where is he that is born king of the Jews? for we have seen his star in the east and are come to worship him. [WISE-MEN *enter from left, bow and stand before* HEROD.] And when he had gathered all the chief priests and scribes of the people together, he demanded of them where Christ should be born. And they said unto him, In Bethlehem of Judæa, for thus it is written by the prophet: And thou Bethlehem, in the land of Juda, art not the least among the princes of Juda: for out of thee shall come a governor that shall rule my people, Israel. [HEROD *rises and points right.*] Then Herod sent them to Bethlehem, saying, go and search diligently for the young child; and when ye have found him, bring me word again, that I may come and worship him also. [WISE-MEN *exit right.*] When they had heard the king they departed; and lo, the star, which they saw in the east, went before them, till it came and stood over where the young child was."

CHOIR OR ORGAN—"Star of the East." [WISE-MEN *make exit by side doors to rear of church, where they remain, ready to advance.*]

SOLOS—"We Three Kings of Orient Are." [*Sung by* WISE-MEN *themselves, or by male soloists in the* CHOIR, *the former being much more effective. While first verse is sung, yellow light floods the stage. When the second verse begins, the first* KING *comes down the aisle with majestic tread, bearing a crown on a cushion lifted high. When he reaches the upper platform he bows low and kneels, laying the crown at feet of mother and Babe, then stands back of manger. Then a second* KING *advances from rear of church, while third verse is sung. He bears high a censer filled with frankincense, and follows actions of the first* KING. *Then, while the fourth verse is sung, the third* KING *advances, bearing a golden casket of myrrh. When all have taken their places behind manger the fifth verse is sung.*]

CHOIR—"As with Gladness Men of Old."

READER—"Behold, the prophet has written, It shall come to pass in the last days that the mountain of the Lord's house shall be established in the top of the mountains, and shall be exalted above the hills; and all nations shall flow unto it. And many people shall go and say, Come ye, and let us go up to the mountain of the Lord; and he will teach us of his ways, and we will walk in his paths; and he shall judge among the nations, and shall rebuke many people; and they shall beat their swords into plowshares, and their spears into pruning-hooks; nation shall not lift up sword against nation, neither shall they learn war any more."

PROCESSIONAL—"Angels from the Realms of Glory" [*all characters and* CHOIR]. [*During this hymn the* REPRE-SENTATIVES OF THE NATIONS *come two by two from rear of church, bearing gifts for the needy. They are led by older boys and girls bearing candles. The latter form an aisle at the altar, through which the* REPRESENTATIVES OF THE NA-TIONS *pass as they ascend to the manger, where they lay their gifts.*]

CHOIR—"Alleluia." [*All children kneel.*]

RECESSIONAL—"Joy to the World" [*all characters and* CHOIR]. [*The* REPRESENTATIVES OF THE NATIONS *lead, fol-lowed by the* KINGS *and then the* SHEPHERDS. *Yellow light fades and blue light comes on again. The* ANGEL *comes down on lower platform.*]

ANGEL—"Jesus said, I am the light of the world; he that followeth me shall not walk in darkness, but shall have the light of life.

[CANDLE BEARERS *approach and kneel in couples;* ANGEL *takes their candles, one at a time, and lights them alternately from right and left of the altar, till all are lighted, while* CHOIR *sings.*]

CHOIR—"Silent Night, Holy Night" [*all verses*]. [*Dur-ing second verse* MARY *lifts the child from manger and exits slowly at right, followed by* JOSEPH. *She turns out light in manger when she removes the Babe.*]

ANGEL—"Ye are the light of the world. Let your light so shine before men that they may see your good works and glorify your father which is in heaven."

ORGAN—"Speed Away." [CANDLE BEARERS *divide to each side and light the candles in windows and elsewhere, then return to altar.*]

ANGEL [*with uplifted arms*]—"The Lord bless thee and keep thee; the Lord make his face to shine upon thee; the Lord lift up the light of his countenance upon thee and give thee peace. Amen."

ORGAN—"Joy to the World" [*while audience leaves*].

184

The Torch Bearers*

A PAGEANT OF MISSIONARY CHALLENGE

CHARACTERS

NARRATOR.
HERALDS OF THE DAWN.
ANGELS OF LIGHT.
PILGRIMS OF THE NIGHT.
WOMEN AND CHILDREN OF THE NATIONS.
CHOIR.

COSTUMES

NARRATOR.

A mature woman in modern dress or white Grecian robe. Carries a scroll upon which her message is printed.

HERALDS.

There should be twenty of these, both men and women being used, if desired. They may wear surplices made of white cloth or crepe paper, reaching about halfway between waist and knees. Veils of orange-colored cheesecloth folded across forehead and hanging down back of neck, the cloth being about one yard long. Each carries a Bible in right hand and a lighted candle in left.

ANGELS.

There should be about sixteen of these, both men and women, in the group, if desired. They also wear white robes with white veils.

---

* Arranged from a pageant of the same title, by Mrs. Mary Isham, published by the Woman's Foreign Missionary Society of the Methodist Episcopal Church, and with the permission of the publishers.

Half of them carry lilies and half carry trumpets, the latter being made by using long rolls of heavy paper covered with gold paper.

PILGRIMS.

There should be forty of these, or just twice as many as the number of HERALDS. They wear black robes, with black scarfs covering head and face.

WOMEN AND CHILDREN OF NATIONS.

Four or more may be used in each group, as desired. See section on "National Costumes."

ARRANGEMENT

The platform should have entrances at each side and broad steps leading from center front. No special scenery is needed, but bright draperies or folding screens make an effective background. The CHOIR may be visible or invisible, as desired.

PAGEANT

NARRATOR—In the beginning God gave the Word— and there was light. How it came, swiftly, instantly, or perhaps by a slow dawning, increasing in brightness until the full glory of the noonday came, we have no record. Day succeeded day through the long years, until the fullness of time was come when God sent His Son into the world. He Himself said, "I am the light of the world. He that followeth after me shall not walk in darkness." He came not to Israel alone, but to Jew and Gentile, bond and free, that all might have the Light of life. When His supreme sacrifice had been accomplished the heavens received Him again. At His passing He left His unfinished task to Peter and John and the other disciples; to Luther and Livingstone; to Carey and Judson and Morrison, and to you and to me—

186

the task of carrying forward the torches which are to light the whole earth—torches, for though a city may flash into light by turning a lever, the Light of life is borne only by the ambassadors of the King. It passes from hand to hand, and flames from heart to heart.

PROCESSIONAL. [CHOIR *sings the "Angel Song" ("Hark, Hark, My Soul") while* ANGELS OF LIGHT *march in couples up the aisles and ascend center steps, then pass to rear of platform. Following them are the* WOMEN AND CHILDREN OF THE NATIONS, *who take their places at front of the platform.*]

RECITATIVE [*by one of the* ANGELS, *who steps forward*] —"Arise, shine, for thy light is come, and the glory of the Lord is risen upon thee," etc. (Isa. 60: 1-9).

NARRATOR [*introducing* WOMEN AND CHILDREN OF THE NATIONS]—More than a century ago the first torch bearer from the Western church entered southern Asia. In India their progress was slow and difficult. India's millions of women were behind high barriers and shrouded in darkness that shut out both the light of the sun and the Light of the world. Under cover of that darkness cruelty ruled. Manu, lawgiver of the Hindu people, fixed the status of women centuries ago. Since then she has been the slave, without redress for wrongs, condemned to ignorance and degradation. Child marriage has been the curse of India. Each child wife, though married to a man, old, crippled, blind, diseased, or even a leper, must worship her husband as a god. When, by reason of age or disease, the husband dies, she is held responsible, and through the centuries her punishment has been almost greater than she could bear. In the old days she might be burned alive on the funeral pyre of her husband. The widow is the object of scorn and hatred. Starvation and abuse are her portion, if she remains in the family home. When that poor shelter fails, she is driven into the street to starve or to find her bread through shame. If the shadow of a widow falls across the pathway of a man, he makes an offering to the idols that he may be purified. Such are the women for whom Christ died. They are waiting for the Light. Long is the list of men and women from America who carried a torch of Light to them; and long is the list of native Hindus who caught the Flame and carried on.

These [*leading forward those in Indian costume*] are representatives of India's daughters, but their faces are the faces of the daughters of the King. For them the darkness is fled away. These are girls from our mission schools. They have proved to their own people that women have minds and souls. This one [*indicating one of the women*], when she returned from the school to her native village, was the only woman there who could read. She gathered the children and taught them. She visited the women and they listened to the gospel story, and for that village Christ is truly the Light of life. This miracle of transformation is taking place all over India. Yet the millions of India are so many, they die so fast, and they beg for the Light.

CHOIR [*including* ANGELS, *if desired*]—"From Greenland's Icy Mountains."

NARRATOR [*introducing Japanese characters*]—Japan held out her hands to the West, and the West heaped them with worldly things. The West trained the sons of the Samurai to build warships and equip armies; and the grandsons of artists work in laboratories and electrical power plants and teach in the schools of Japan all the philosophies, doubts and skepticisms of Western atheists. Torch bearers went also, and hundreds and thousands of Japanese worship Christ alone. They are brave, loyal, devoted Christians. Yet in beautiful Japan but one in fifty has ever heard the gospel message. Japan stretches forth her hands for the true Light.

CHOIR—"Ye Christian Heralds."

NARRATOR [*indicating Korean girls*]—These represent the people of Korea who, a generation ago, were the "Hermit Nation." The women were shut up in the close little houses, never leaving them except for the single hour when the streets were given over to them. Passing through the streets at any other hours, you would hear the steady tap, tap, tap of the ironing sticks as the women polished the immaculate white suits in which the man of Korea delights to array himself. Fifty years ago the first torch bearers entered Korea, and within the first three years seven converts were baptized. Today there are thousands of Korean Christians, and the missionaries are overwhelmed in the floodtide of opportunities. These eager Korean Christians love our Christ and His Word. They are loving, praying, generous Christians, so eager to pass the Torch to others that they tithe not only money, but time, in His service. They have sent messengers to their countrymen in the Pacific Islands, in Manchuria and Siberia, and their hearts go out to the great Chinese Empire.

CHOIR—"Speed Away."

NARRATOR—These girls in their gay, soft colors, are from Burma, land of Buddhists. There are no zenanas in Burma, and women are perhaps more free than in any other Oriental land. Yet in the religion of Buddha there is no place for women in the eightfold path which leads to peace. Perhaps because of that they are all the more ready to turn from the debasing worship of the priests to the Christ, who saves even women, and makes no distinction between them and their brothers.

CHOIR—"Jesus Saves."

NARRATOR—Here are African women and children. "Ethiopia shall stretch out her hands to God," was the promise made long ago, and that promise is being fulfilled today. The continent of mystery has been unveiled, and the paths to the interior are marked by the graves of the torch bearers. The past decade has shown wonderful progress in African missions. The turning of these primitive peoples from fetishism and superstitions of witch doctors and charms, calls for supreme devotion. God gives to those who volunteer for Africa blessings commensurate with their sacrifice. Yet today, as of old, Africa is in darkness. Today she stands at the parting of the ways. Christ or Mohammed? It shall be as the churches of the West decree. There are a hundred million people without a written language or even an alphabet. There are, after more than a century of modern missions, fifty millions of people in Africa outside the reach of even the plans of any missionary society.

CHOIR—"Send the Light."

NARRATOR—These with veiled faces are representatives of the Moslem world. They come from Arabia, Palestine, Syria, Turkey, Africa, Persia and India. The length and breadth of the Orient knows the smothering folds of the Moslem veil. Mohammedans worship God and Mohammed, but reject the Saviour of men. They prate of brotherhood and enslave their women. The prophet made no place for women in his scheme of government and religion, save that of slavery and degradation. Enslaved by the veil and the harem, child marriage, polygamy, divorce, with no place even in the mosque for worship, the daughters of Hagar, an endless procession, make their way to hopeless graves. In Mohammedanism, Christianity meets its greatest foe, for it is sweeping millions into its grip, and Moslems are the most difficult of all people to evangelize.

CHOIR—"We've a Story to Tell to the Nations."

NARRATOR—No one needs to be told that these are the daughters of China. Their clear eyes declare them the daughters of new China. Looking at them and at the hundreds of bright, lovable girls in our Chinese mission schools, our hearts are lifted up. But looking beyond this line of Christian pioneers we see great provinces with hundreds of thousands who have never heard that there is a Saviour. And how shall they hear? There are in China nearly 500,000 people to each Protestant minister. The church universal was aroused and thrilled when ten thousand Chinese Christians went to death rather than deny Christ.

CHOIR—"Hail to the Brightness."

NARRATOR—Now, as never in the history of nations, the whole earth is waiting for the coming of the Light. Every land has opened its doors and has servants ready to receive the Torch.

CHOIR—"The Morning Light Is Breaking." [REPRE-SENTATIVES OF THE NATIONS *march from the platform during this song.*]

NARRATOR—"The Torch."

> Pass on the torch, pass on the flame;
> Remember whence the Glory came,
> And eyes are on you as you run,
> Beyond the shining of the sun!
>
> Lord Christ, we take the torch from Thee!
> We must be true, we will be free;
> And clean of heart and strong of soul,
> To bear the Glory to its goal.
>
> O Lord of life, to Thee we kneel;
> Maker of men, our purpose seal!
> We will, for honor of Thy name,
> Pass on the torch, pass on the flame.

> *—Allen Eastman Cross.*

CHOIR—"O Zion, Haste." [*Lights should be dimmed, while* PILGRIMS OF THE NIGHT *advance, one by one, from the left, meeting* HERALDS OF THE DAWN, *who come from the right. Each* HERALD *gives Bible to* PILGRIM *when they meet in center of stage, takes her hand and leads her down the steps and center aisle, allowing space between couples. When the last* HERALD *has gone, the remaining* PILGRIMS *keep on advancing to platform until all are assembled. They turn, seeking the light, groping with outstretched hands, appealingly, and one may fall. Then all turn and make their uncertain way out into the darkness from which they came.*]

CHOIR [*and audience, if desired*]—"Christ for the World, We Sing."

BENEDICTION.

Uncle Sam's Family

A PAGEANT OF AMERICA AND HER PEOPLE

CHARACTERS

UNCLE SAM.	JAPANESE GIRL.
AN INDIAN.	CHINESE BOY.
NEGRO.	PORTO RICAN.
HIGHLANDER.	EUROPEAN.
MEXICAN.	CHOIR.

COSTUMES

UNCLE SAM.

Customary suit of red-and-white striped trousers, bright-blue coat with white stars, and tall hat. This suit may be purchased at a reasonable price from Paine Publishing Co., Dayton, O.

OTHER CHARACTERS.

See section of "National Costumes."

ARRANGEMENT

Special scenery is not necessary, but the platform may be draped with flags and ferns, and flowers may be placed here and there.

The speeches should be given out in advance, so they may be memorized. If desired, there may be several characters in each group, and they may be introduced by UNCLE SAM, who tells in third person who they are, reading from a book with paper cover on which "My Family" is printed.

PAGEANT

ORGAN AND TRUMPETS WITH CHOIR—"God of Our Fathers, Whose Almighty Hand."

UNCLE SAM [*coming to center of platform*]—

"God be merciful unto us, and bless us;
And cause his face to shine upon us;
That thy way may be known upon earth,
Thy salvation among all nations.
Let the peoples praise thee, O God;
Let all the peoples praise thee.
Oh let the nations be glad and sing for joy;
For thou wilt judge the peoples with equity,
And govern the nations upon earth.
Praise the Lord, O Jerusalem;
Praise thy God, O Zion,
For he hath strengthened the bars of thy gates;
He hath blessed thy children within thee.
He maketh peace in thy borders;
And filleth thee with the finest of the wheat.
He hath not dealt so with any nation."

CHOIR AND AUDIENCE—"America the Beautiful."

UNCLE SAM—Dear friends of our United States, I am glad to welcome you all to our reception this evening, so that we may, with true American hospitality, greet the special representatives of our great family. Zangwill's term, "the melting pot," applies well to this country. Within our broad borders all the races of the world come together and are fused into a civilization the like of which the world has never seen. Our population is becoming marked by the good qualities of all human races, and it also has a chance to be marred by their bad qualities. They have much to contribute to the higher life of our country, and we have a great responsibility to them. With Christian brotherhood in our hearts we can develop a nation that will be blessed by God, who sent His only Son that there might be "peace on earth, good will toward men."

CHOIR—"My Own United States" [*or other special patriotic song*].

UNCLE SAM—As the people of this great country have affectionately dubbed me their "Uncle," I am happy tonight to preside at this reception and hope every one will be attentive to our representatives. First we will hear from the Indians.

INDIAN—I am a *real* American—some call me the *first* American. I did not come here. I have always been here. I was the custodian of this great land before the march of history brought the white man here. I have helped make America what it is. I helped the pioneer find his way. Some of our great modern highways over the wide plains, through the mountains and across the desert follow my ancient trails. Sometimes when I have been mistreated or have not understood, I have fought for my freedom, but for the most part I have been the white man's friend. I gave him corn and the potato. I kept him from starvation and was the guest at his first Thanksgiving. My brothers by the thousand, as scouts, have given their lives for our country. We have always feared and worshiped God, whom we called the Great Spirit. But I need to be taught and trained in the ways of true democracy, industry and co-operation, for I have been misled and have many wrong conceptions. I want to help build the new America by becoming self-reliant, industrious, and worthy of respect and honor. There are 350,000 of my people in Uncle Sam's family—full-fledged citizens by vote of Congress—but we want to be real citizens in mind and heart.

CHOIR—"God Bless Our Native Land."

NEGRO—I also am a loyal American, and one out of every nine members of Uncle Sam's family have my blood in their veins. I came to America, not because I wanted to, but because I had to. My grandfathers and grandmothers were slaves, but the great Lincoln set them free, and today I am a free citizen. I have done much to build the new America, not only by the enforced labor of my hands in the past, but by my voluntary service and sacrifice in every time of need. In every one of America's great struggles for liberty and justice I have been in the front line. My blood was the first to be shed in the American Revolution, and many of my brothers gave their lives in the great World War. I *love* America and want her to be great and good. And I believe that I can help make her so with my music, my art, my literature, my industry, my self-control, my passionate love of justice which was born out of great tribulation, and my faith in God.

CHOIR—"Steal Away to Jesus" [*or other spiritual*].

HIGHLANDER—I come from the mountains of the South. My relatives number three millions. It is said that I have the purest blood in my veins of any group in America. Abraham Lincoln belonged to my group, and he is our greatest gift to America. I come offering my fearlessness, my mountain sturdiness, the pure blood, simple faith and unspoiled life of the mountaineer. Give me a chance and I, with my ambitious brothers and promising sisters, will help build into the America of the future the strength of our eternal hills. I am a little behind some of my fellow Americans, but I have a future, and one wise man said, "A backward ancestor may be better than a degenerating grandson."

CHOIR—"For the Beauty of the Earth" [*vs.* 1 *and* 2].

MEXICAN—I represent the Spanish-speaking citizens of the United States. There are about two millions of us, besides those in Porto Rico. I am helping build America by my labor in the cotton fields and the fruit ranches, in the mines, on the railroads and along the great highways. But I can bring to America, along with the labor of my hands, my joy in life, my light-heartedness and my love of beauty. Some Americans say they do not want me, and would close the gates against me, but I, too, seek the opportunity which our country offers to better my own condition and to give my children the chance to learn.

CHOIR—"I Heard the Voice of Jesus Say."

JAPANESE GIRL—I am one of 110,000 Japanese living mostly on the Pacific Coast, the shores nearest my native land. There are also 100,000 more of us in Hawaii. I am helping make the new America with my hands. I am transforming the great American desert into a garden, making fruit, vegetables and flowers to grow where once there were only waste places. Some people say, "Keep America white," but my people are trying to make it green. I bring skill and toil and beauty from the land of the cherry blossom. More than a third of all my people were born in the United States and love America as you do.

CHINESE BOY—I come hand in hand with my Japanese sister to do my part in building the new America. I have helped my Mexican brother build our mines and railroads and highways. I also am helping to feed America and to keep her clean. But I have better gifts to offer. I bring the spirit of obedience, reverence for the past, patient industry and toil in the face of difficulty and discouragement. There are 62,000 of us in Uncle Sam's family, but most of the young people are American citizens by birth.

CHOIR—"In Christ There Is No East or West."

PORTO RICAN—I am the youngest of Uncle Sam's family, but not the smallest, for there are over a million of us. I

was adopted by Uncle Sam, but I am glad to be an adopted
child, and I want to do my share to make the home of all
of us beautiful, friendly and truly Christian. During a terrible hurricane which visited our island, some of my sisters,
who were nurses at the Ryder Memorial Hospital, showed
that they could be just as brave and helpful as their teachers.
I can help America not only by giving her coffee and sweeten-
ing it for breakfast, but by working with Uncle Sam for
better health, better education and better homes.

CHOIR—"There's a Wideness in God's Mercy."

EUROPEAN—I represent many millions of my European
brothers and sisters who are a part of Uncle Sam's great
family. We began coming with the Pilgrim Fathers and
have kept coming nearly every year by hundreds. Every
country of Europe is represented in our group, and we have
brought some of the most loyal citizens which America ever
welcomed. And we have brought a heritage of devotion, of
industry, of intelligence and of loyalty. We have furnished
many of Uncle Sam's laborers, scientists, doctors, musicians,
poets, inventors, novelists and dramatists. Our contribution
of talent and service is woven into the very fabric of our nation's life. We plead for friendship and Christian teaching.

CHOIR—"Faith of Our Fathers."

UNCLE SAM [standing in center of his family group,
whose heads are bowed]—

> God bless our dear United States,
> Preserve the land from evil fates,
> Lift high her banner fair and free,
> And guard her bounds from sea to sea.
>
> From foe without and foe within,
> From open shame and hidden sin,
> From boastful pride and greedy store,
> God keep our nation evermore.

Forever may her friendly hands
Receive the poor of others lands
In kindliness of sisterhood,
And fill their arms with ample good.

Assailed by battle hosts of wrong,
God help our country to be strong,
Assailed by falsehood's crafty crew,
God help our country to be true.

God hold the nation's aim sincere,
God save her heart from cowardly fear,
God prosper her in true success,
And crown her head with worthiness.

God bless our dear United States,
Preserve the land from evil fates,
Lift high her banner fair and free,
And ever guard her liberty.
        —*"The People's Prayer," by Amos R. Wells.*
    (Used by permission of the *Christian Endeavor World,*
        in which it was first published.)

CHOIR, CHARACTERS AND AUDIENCE—"America."

National Costumes

Because several of the pageants in this text include characters representing the various nations, it is believed that this section will be helpful in planning costumes without further research.

MATERIAL

Costumes need not be expensive, and in many cases may be made from remnants of cloth and old garments found in many homes. Pieces of bright cloth make excellent turbans, shawls, capes and girdles. When long skirts are worn by the girls, they may wear their modern shoes. When short skirts are worn, they may wear bedroom slippers, which also may be worn by the boys. Blue overall trousers, knickers and white trousers may be worn by the boys representing many of the nations, with ordinary shirts arranged as blouses.

ASIA

CHINA

Men—Pajamas of plain color, with fancy decorations, and a small black hat of fez style for men of average rank. Blue overall trousers and coat, with large straw hat, for a coolie.

Women—Pajamas of plain colors, with straight, black hair, heavily oiled.

JAPAN

Men—Dark kimono, with sleeves gathered at wrist and narrow girdle.

Women—Bright kimono, with wide silk girdle, tied at the back to form a large, flat bow. Black hair, combed tight and decorated with pom-poms or other ornaments.

KOREA

Men—White trousers, with a sheet draped to represent a double-breasted coat, reaching halfway between knees and ankles. Large, black hat of "sugar-loaf" style, made from cardboard and tied under the chin.

Women—Long, full skirt, fastened high under the arms, and made of any light, pale color; the waist is of a contrasting color, made in jacket style, tied in front, and having long sleeves.

INDIA

Men—Each caste has a characteristic costume (which also is true of the women). The poorer class would wear a long, white strip wrapped around the waist and hanging to ankles, with chest and arms bare. The higher class would wear a costume similar to Korean men, with coat reaching just below the knees, and a heavily coiled turban.

Women—Short, tight-sleeved jacket of bright color. The skirt should be of a contrasting color and made from several yards of cloth wrapped around the limbs, with one end draped under the left arm and over the head to make a *sari*, or scarf.

BURMA

Men—Costume similar to men of India, with a red, fez-shaped hat.

Women—Costume similar to the women of India, without the *sari*. Beads and bracelets may be worn. Material for the skirt should be of stripes which run horizontally.

CEYLON

Men—Costume similar to men of India (higher caste), with turban of bright material.

Women—Costume similar to women of India. Their black, glossy hair is parted and adorned with many elaborate silver ornaments. They also wear bracelets, necklaces and rings.

SIAM

Men—Class here also governs the dress, but the average costume would be pajama style, with the trousers of three-quarter length, and sandals. Broad-brimmed straw hat.

Women—Bright skirt of three-quarter length, with blouse of contrasting color. Beads and bracelets.

ANAM

Men—Long, black trousers. Chemise of brilliant cloth, richly embroidered, reaching to knees (silk dressing gown will do), with no girdle. Small, silk turban.

Women—Costume similar to the men. Their black, glossy hair is adorned with ornaments.

MALAY PENINSULA

Men and Women—Costumes similar to Burma and Siam.

FORMOSA

Men and Women—Costumes similar to low-caste Indians (Hindus).

SYRIA

Men—Dark, baggy trousers, tucked into high boots. White shirt, with wide, brilliant girdle. Long, striped robe. Large turban of bright colors. Mustache.

Women—Long, flowing robe of striped material, with girdle. Strip of dark cloth encircling head, with top uncovered. Earrings, beads and bracelets.

ARABIA

Men—Outing-flannel night dress for tunic; over this a long, open cloak of wide-striped material. Red turban. Mustache.

Women—White skirt, three-quarter length, trimmed with three rows of colored braid near hem. Overskirt of black sateen, open at front, with bright cord hanging down front from belt. White waist with striped collar hanging over sleeves. Head scarf of striped material about one yard square; one side is drawn across forehead and fastened at back of neck, the other three sides hanging in irregular folds; beaded or jeweled ornament on front of scarf. Bare legs, with sandals, and beaded anklets.

PERSIA

Men—Dark, full trousers and dark shirt, with collar turned in. Bright kimono coat, fastened to waist at the back, but loose in front. Small turban of bright cloth.

Women—The chadar, which always is worn in the presence of men, is a long, capelike garment, fastened to a cap, with holes cut for eyes and nose. City women use bright colors in stripes or flowered designs, while village women wear white or plain colors.

TURKESTAN

Men—White shirt and trousers, with brilliant scarf for girdle. Long cloak of gay stripes, open at front. White turban. Dark beard and mustache.

Women—Long, dark cloak swathing the body. Black veil covering head and face. Heavy silver necklaces (tinfoil), bracelets, rings and earrings.

AFGHANISTAN, BALUCHISTAN AND BOKHARA

Men—White, baggy trousers gathered at the ankles. Long, white shirt, with colored girdle and sash. Coat of "smock" style (plain or striped). Tall, brimless hat of colored cloth. Beard and mustache.

Women—Trousers like the men. Cloak of smock style. Dark veil around head and covering face.

PALESTINE

Men—Long cloak of bright stripes, with silken girdle concealing the undergarments. Coiled turban of bright colors. Beard and mustache.

Women—Long skirt and full blouse of mixed colors, the blouse being heavily embroidered. Heavy beads, with coins predominating. The hat is of cylinder shape, eight inches high, made of cardboard or buckram; over this a white embroidered cloth or towel is draped and pinned under the chin, with ends hanging over arms to elbows.

EUROPE

RUSSIA

Men—Dark trousers tucked into high-laced boots or leggings, with baggy arrangement at knees. Dark-blue shirt, with tails outside trousers and girded with leather belt. Dark cape hanging from back of the shoulders. High fur cap. Mustache.

Women—Orange or red skirt, three-quarter length. Small, black apron. White waist with black, sleeveless jacket.

White stockings and black slippers. Headdress of white organdie or linen one-half yard square and pinned in place over ears. Bracelets and earrings.

HUNGARY

Men—Trousers of white muslin, resembling a very full skirt reaching to the shoe tops and trimmed with coarse cotton lace on lower hem. White blouse, with stripe of colored braid down sleeves. Long, narrow, black apron trimmed with zigzags of colored braid. Black hat (straw or velvet), trimmed with artificial flowers.

Women—Bright skirt (yellow preferred), with wide lace on bottom edge. White blouse, with sleeveless jacket of same material as skirt. Black cambric apron, trimmed with fancy braid. White stockings and dark shoes. Funnel-shaped hood twelve inches long, made of buckram or cardboard, covered with flowered cretonne and trimmed with a four-inch fringe on top.

GERMANY

Men—Blue knickers, with white stockings and black slippers. White shirt, with red sleeveless sweater. Blue kerchief knotted at the throat. White "stocking" cap.

Women—Full skirt of bright color, reaching below knees; long, narrow, white apron. White waist with full-length sleeves; black bodice with red laces. White stockings and black slippers. Black skull cap, with huge bow of wide, black ribbon in front, leaving long streamer ends. Imitation yellow hair braids hang at back (made of rope dyed yellow).

FRANCE

Men—Striped trousers and a blue smock similar to that worn by an artist, only shorter. Blue cap in tam-o'-shanter style.

Women—Bright-colored skirt of three-quarter length, with blouse of contrasting color. Lace cap. Bright stockings and black slippers.

SWITZERLAND

Men—Short, green pants, with green suspender straps and a green strap across chest. White shirt, with flowing yellow tie. Small, dark coat. Golf hose, leaving knees bare. Felt hat (green preferred), with brim turned up at sides and a bunch of feathers or flowers sticking up at one side.

Women—Very full skirt of striped material, green and yellow predominating, the stripes running crosswise and the skirt reaching below the knees. Tight waist of black velvet or sateen, made with V-shaped neck, full sleeves and a plaited ruffle at belt line. Small, square, white apron. Bright stockings with black slippers. Felt hat, with brim turned up at sides and a small plume at back.

ITALY

Men—Full, white knee trousers and white shirt. Vest of bright color, with brass buttons. Yellow cloth girdle. Red kerchief around neck. Large, floppy, black hat with low crown, bound with bright ribbon. Bright stockings and black slippers.

Women—Full, red or yellow skirt, with a band of contrasting color six inches from hem. Square apron of various colors. White waist with black bodice. Red kerchief around neck and folded across breast. Square of white cloth made into cap effect and hanging at back of neck. White stockings and black slippers.

HOLLAND

Men—Baggy, blue trousers reaching nearly to ankles. Bright-colored shirt or tight-fitting jacket. Red kerchief around neck. Red socks, with wooden shoes or bright slippers. Bright cap. Golden hair.

Women—Full, blue skirt of three-quarter length. Bright-red waist with black bodice. White apron. Bright stockings, with wooden shoes or bright slippers. White cap with pointed horns. Golden hair.

SPAIN

Men—Black trousers, white shirt, with collar open flat and red kerchief around neck. Wide girdle of bright colors, with sash at side. Large, black hat with stiff brim and soft velvet crown. Scarf of bright colors may be worn over left shoulder.

Women—Full skirt of black sateen reaching below knees and having borders of red, yellow and blue stripes near hem. White waist with short sleeves. Bright silk or embroidered shawl, with fringed edges, is tucked in belt at front. White stockings and black slippers. Headdress of black lace (mantilla) draped over large comb and hanging down back of neck. Heavy bracelets, earrings and brooches.

PORTUGAL

Men—Long trousers of black or brown, with high vest and short coat. Red girdle with sash. Large felt hat.

Women—Short, full skirt of black sateen, with broad stripe of bright color above the hem. White blouse, with small, black, sleeveless jacket. White stockings and black slippers. Kerchief-draped head topped with wide-brimmed, black hat.

DENMARK

Men—Knee-length trousers, with long, dark stockings. Low shoes, with large, silver buckles. Dark shirt, with bright bow tie. Short coat and jaunty cap.

Women—Dark, full skirt of three-quarter length. Waist of same or contrasting material, with laced bodice. Light apron, with crosswise embroidery decorations. Small, fringed shawl. Black bonnet, with long streamers tied under chin.

NORWAY

Men—Black or brown trousers tucked into plaid golf hose at knees. Black slippers. Vest like trousers, with bright necktie. White coat, trimmed with gold braid and buttons. Felt hat, with flat crown and bright ribbon band.

Women—Skirt of dark material (blue, green or brown) reaching to shoe tops. White apron (knee length and one foot wide), with border and edge of fancy braid or lace. White waist with long sleeves. Black, sleeveless jacket, trimmed with white rick-rack braid. Headdress of white linen or Swiss, wired or starched to form a half-circle "halo" from ear to ear. White stockings and black slippers.

SWEDEN

Men—Dark trousers tucked into cream-colored hose at knees; black slippers. Bright-blue coat (denim farm coat will do), with collar turned up around throat. Orange ribbon around neck. Bell-shaped cap of wool or fur.

Women—Skirt of dark material reaching to shoe tops. White muslin apron trimmed with vertical stripes of blue, yellow and green. White blouse, with bolero-style jacket of black and laced across breast. Cap of yellow and black, puffed. White stockings, black slippers.

RUMANIA

Men—Close-fitting wool or linen trousers. Plain shirt, with bright vest. White tunic reaching to knees (an old night shirt or gown, open down the front, will do). Broad, black, felt hat. Mustache.

Women—Bright, embroidered skirt, three-quarter length. White, embroidered blouse. Brilliant tunic of knee length (a fancy dressing gown). White stockings and shoes. White scarf wound around head, with one end hanging at the back.

BULGARIA

Men—White trousers and shirt. Wide girdle of brilliant silk, with sash. Black sateen jacket reaching below hips, with elbow sleeves, leaving sleeves of white shirt show below. This jacket is open in front and is richly embroidered. Black cap of "fez" shape. Dark mustache.

Women—White, embroidered dress of knee length, with long sleeves. A shorter overdress of dark cloth, and sleeves of elbow length; this garment has a low neck to show the white undergarment. Narrow aprons of horizontal stripes, one worn in front and one in back. Bright kerchief over head and pinned at back of neck. Bright stockings and low shoes. Many necklaces of coins.

ALBANIA

Men—Baggy, white or colored woolen trousers, tight at ankles. White shirt, with baggy sleeves at wrists. Black bolero jacket, richly embroidered. Red girdle with sash. Short, black, wool coat, with elbow-length sleeves, fringed. White felt fez. Long, silver chain (tinfoil) around neck.

Women—Baggy trousers like men, but of bright colors. Brilliant embroidered waist, with high collar and cuff sleeves. Brilliant girdle. Dark lace cap, with ends hanging at back. Many jewels.

TURKEY

Men—Red sateen trousers, baggy at hips, but tight from knees down. White shirt, with black jacket having long sleeves. Wide, green girdle. Red fez having a long, black tassel.

Women—Bloomer-style skirt of purple sateen, ankle length. Blouse of striped material, with wide girdle. Turban of striped material. Veil of black lace or net across nose and tied at back of head, thus covering the mouth. Beads around neck.

GREECE

Men—Large, baggy trousers of dark material. White blouse. Scarlet vest, with brilliant embroidery. Red fez, with blue tassel.

Women—White or light-blue skirt, with deep embroidery at lower hem. Square apron of brilliant colors. Blouse like skirt, with decorated sleeves. Sleeveless cloak of bright colors, open in front, with embroidered edges and of three-quarter length. Cheesecloth scarf draped around head and throat. Heavy beads.

CZECHO-SLOVAKIA

(Moravia, Bohemia, Silesia, Slovakia)

Men—Dark trousers trimmed with white rick-rack braid and tucked into high boots or leggings. White blouse with high collar. Bolero-style jacket (sleeveless) of orange sateen, edged with black. Black, bell-shaped cap, with bunch of bright flowers on one side.

Women—Skirt of dark material, reaching just below knees. Square apron of white muslin, trimmed with braid and lace. White blouse with wide, open collar and deep lace on elbow-length sleeves. Black sleeveless jacket. Cap of white cheesecloth, puffed high, with ends hanging at back of neck.

(To feature the four provinces, the men may be distinguished by beards and mustaches and jackets of different colors, while the women are distinguished by their queer-shaped hats and bonnets.)

JUGO-SLAVIA

(Croatia, Servia, Bosnia, Montenegro, Dalmatia, Slovenia)

Men—White trousers and shirt. Short, red waistcoat. Nine-inch leather belt. Long, linen smock. Broad felt hat. Dark mustache.

Women—Smocklike linen tunic of ankle length, with large sleeves. Brilliant jacket without sleeves. Bright embroidered apron. Head shawl of blue, violet or rose cloth. Many strings of beads.

(To feature the six provinces, the men may wear capes and hats of different colors, while the women have queer bonnets, aprons and shawls.)

LAPLAND

Men—Knee-length trousers with leggings. Wool shirt, with long, wool jacket girded at the waist. High cap with "bill" in front and a fur pom-pom on top, at rear.

Women—Wool skirt of three-quarter length. Waist of lumber-jacket style. Dark stockings with high shoes. High cap of blue and scarlet cloth. Large glass beads.

FINLAND

Men—Dark trousers wrapped with cords from ankles to knees. Overcoat or heavy raincoat of knee length. Dark blouse. High-crowned felt hat.

Women—Skirt of striped material, three-quarter length. Black apron richly embroidered. Brilliant blouse with black bodice. Kerchief on head and tied under chin. Dark stockings and shoes.

ESTONIA

Men—Dark trousers with leggings and dark blouse. Heavy coat like Finnish neighbor. Cap with visor.

Women—Skirt of striped material, three-quarter length, with embroidered apron. Long-sleeved embroidered blouse with black bodice. Large brooch at throat and many necklaces. High, pointed hat, with red-and-white checkered kerchief tied over it and fastened under chin. White stockings and dark slippers.

POLAND

Men—Dark trousers tucked into boots or leggings. Long, smocklike shirt girded at waist with leather belt. Felt hat.

Women—Short, ruffled skirt of dark, striped material. White blouse, with embroidered sleeveless jacket. Straight apron of plain cloth. Many strands of amber and coral beads. Bright head shawl. Dark stockings and shoes.

SCOTLAND

Men—Skirt of plaid gingham reaching above knees. Plaid golf hose rolled below knees, leaving knees bare. Black slippers. White shirt, with short jacket of blue or green, and a red tie. Sash of plaid cloth over left shoulder. Cap of dough-boy style (creased through center), with feather at side.

Women—Dress of plain color (full skirt), with plaid shawl (gingham or calico). Tam-o'-shanter hat. White stockings and black slippers.

IRELAND

Men—Tan or brown knee-length trousers, with black stockings rolled up over trousers. Black slippers. White shirt with flowing green tie. Green vest and brown coat. Brown hat with green band.

Women—Use girls with reddish hair and blue eyes. Full, green skirt. White waist with low neck and elbow sleeves. Red girdle. Shawl or kerchief of green-plaid gingham, with ends tucked into girdle. Bright stockings and slippers. Broad-brimmed straw hat with ribbon strings.

WALES

Men—Old-fashioned dark suit, with high white collar and felt hat.

Women—Old-fashioned black dress, with white apron and fancy flowered shawl. "Sugar-loaf" hat with wide brim, made from black cardboard.

MEDITERRANEAN ISLANDS

CORSICA

Men—Modern American trousers and vest. White shirt, with bright necktie. Cap with visor.

Women—Modern dress, with elbow-length sleeves. Large, floppy hat.

SARDINIA

Men—White knee breeches, very baggy, and white blouse. Black stockings or leggings. Brown embroidered jacket (sleeveless) covering hips. Blue scarf tied into a turban, with ends hanging at back of neck.

Women—Long, full skirt of brilliant colors. White blouse, with brilliant eton jacket. Bright kerchief on head and tied under chin.

SICILY

Men—Blue or brown trousers. Colored shirt with fancy vest. Wide girdle of bright silk. Small turban hat.

Women—Full skirt of brilliant color, with eton jacket. White blouse with very full sleeves. Wide gilded belt with large buckle. Ribbon around hair.

CRETE

Men—Baggy trousers of dark material and white shirt. Vest of bright color, heavily embroidered. Tall hat of bright silk.

Women—Light skirt, three-quarter length, with deep embroidery. Square apron of bright material. Light blouse, with embroidery on the sleeves. Lace cap.

AFRICA

EGYPT

Men—Long, coatlike garment, similar to that of Arabians, with bright girdle and sash. Red fez with blue tassel.

Women—Large cloak of dark material which almost envelops the body. Turban of white cheesecloth, with one end over face for veil.

MOROCCO, ALGERIA, TRIPOLI

Men—Wrapped in creamy, white wool or cotton cloak (a sheet will do). White turban with hood effect and crossed under chin.

Women—Similar to men, but cloth of pale color. Beads and bracelets.

(To distinguish the three countries, men of Algeria wear colored turban, and men of Tripoli have striped cloak over the white. All may wear dark mustache and short beard.)

CONGO STATE, CAPE COLONY, LIBERIA, NIGERIA, KAMERUN, ANGOLA

Men—Caste and country, of course, have some effect on the dress, but an average costume of a native would be short, ragged trousers and a plain shirt. Turbans of bright cloth and old hats may be worn as distinguishing features. If white people are used, they should wear brown stockings on legs and arms, and have faces darkened with cocoa.

Women—Skirt of bright color, fastened high under arms and reaching below knees. Waist of plain material, with short sleeves. Arms, legs and face prepared like the men, if white people are used.

ABYSSINIA AND RHODESIA

Men—Strip of dark cloth wrapped around body, making both trousers and shirt, with arms bare. Small, bright turban. Mustache.

Women—Costume similar to women of other states of Africa.

AUSTRALASIAN COLONIES

TASMANIA, NEW GUINEA, NEW ZEALAND

Men—Dark-skinned, with long strip of cloth wrapped around body, forming both trousers and shirt, leaving arms bare.

Women—Similar to men, with lower part arranged as a skirt. Ornaments in black hair.

EAST INDIES

JAVA, SUMATRA, BORNEO

Men—Dark-skinned, with knee-length overall trousers and plain shirts. Broad-brimmed straw hats.

Women—Dark-skinned, with long strip of bright cloth wrapped around body, forming both skirt and waist, with arms bare. Ornaments, beads and bracelets.

SOUTH SEA ISLANDS

NEW HEBRIDES, NEW CALEDONIA, SAMOA, FIJI, SOLOMON

Men—Dark-skinned, with long strip of cloth wrapped around body, forming both trousers and shirt, leaving arms bare.

Women—Dark-skinned, with short, fluffy skirt of flowered material, and cloth of contrasting color wrapped around chest and back, forming a waist, with arms bare. Wreath of flowers around head. Necklaces of shell beads.

HAWAII

Men—Dark-skinned, with modern, light summer suit and broad straw hat.

Women—Dark-skinned, with fluffy dress of light, flowered cloth, and wreath of flowers around head. Necklaces and bracelets.

PHILIPPINES

Men—Dark-skinned, with linen or Palm Beach suit and broad straw hat.

Women—Dark-skinned, with long skirt of bright silk and net overskirt of three-quarter length. Waist of light material, with large lace sleeves and low neck. Glossy, black hair, coiled high. Necklace, bracelets, fancy fan and parasol.

WEST INDIES

CUBA AND PORTO RICO

Men—Modern Palm Beach suit, with Mexican straw hat. Dark-skinned.

Women—Modern, light dress, with brilliant silk shawl.

HAITI, JAMAICA AND SANTO DOMINGO

Men—Negro complexion. Overall trousers with suspenders over a bright shirt. Big straw hat.

Women—Plain, cotton dress of light colors and small straw hat. Negro complexion.

NORTH AMERICA

MEXICO

Men—Tight, black trousers (velour or corduroy). White shirt, with flowing, blue tie. Tight, red jacket (trimmed with gilt braid, if possible). Typical broad-brimmed Mexican hat. Black or brown slippers. Dark mustache.

Women—Full skirt and waist of bright color, with girdle and sash of contrasting colors, and bright shawl. Bright scarf tied around head, with ends hanging at back of neck. Bright stockings and slippers; earrings, beads and bracelets.

ALASKA (AND GREENLAND)

Men—Heavy, knee-length trousers, with leggings. Buckskin or fur coat, or knit sweater with design. Long, straight hair, with fur cap. Skin of Indian-Negro appearance.

Women—Similar to men, except that hair is braided.

AMERICAN INDIANS

Men—Brown cambric or khaki trousers or overalls; bright wool shirt; blanket, and headdress of feathers. For Indians of modern days, a cap or felt hat is worn, instead of the feathers.

Women—For pioneer days the dress was a plain, dark slip, with one feather at back of head and a blanket around shoulders. For modern days they wear bright dresses with full skirts and sleeves. Many beads and bracelets.

PURITANS

Men—Dark suit with knee breeches, a wide, leather belt being worn outside the coat, the latter reaching below the hips. Collar of shirt is spread flat, outside coat. Cape of dark cloth. White hose with dark slippers which have large buckles. Hat of "sugar-loaf" style.

Women—Long, dark dress. White apron and white kerchief around shoulders. Long, dark cape. Dark hood tied under chin, with streamer bows.

SOUTH AMERICA

The twelve countries of this continent have costumes which are combinations of Spanish, Portuguese, Mexican dress. Each may be featured in a large pageant.

CENTRAL AMERICA

The several countries of this nation also have combinations of other nations in their costumes, including the Spanish, Mexican and American Indian. Each may be featured in a large pageant.

Index to Song Sources

KEY TO NAMES OF SONGBOOKS

C H	Christian Hymnal. (The Standard Publishing Co.)
F H	Favorite Hymns. (The Standard Publishing Co.)
F S	Favorite Solos. (The Standard Publishing Co.)
G B	Golden Book of Favorite Songs. (Hall & McCreary Co.)
J H	A Junior Hymnal. (The Standard Publishing Co.)
M D	Mother's Day Book No. 2. (The Standard Publishing Co.)
N C	New Church Hymnal. (Hope Publishing Co.)
N P	New Praise Hymnal. (Fillmore Brothers Co.)
S C H	Standard Church Hymns and Gospel Songs. (Rodeheaver Publishing Co.)
S C B	Standard Christmas Book No. 2. (The Standard Publishing Co.)
S P	Songs of Praises. (The Standard Publishing Co.)
S S	Sociability Songs. (The Standard Publishing Co.)
S S D	Sacred Solos and Duets No. 1. (The Standard Publishing Co.)
W B	World's Best Christmas Carols. (The Standard Publishing Co.)

TITLES OF SONGS

A Charge to Keep I Have_____ F H
A Mighty Fortress Is Our God_____ F H
Alas! and Did My Saviour Bleed?_____ F H

220

Index to Song Sources

221

Index to Song Sources

Index to Song Sources

Index to Song Sources